Physical C
Hu
(from The Ke

Body: Withers slightly higher than level of back, which is of medium length. Loin short and broad, belly slightly tucked up. Ribs deep, rib cage broadening from behind elbows and well sprung. Rump short and slightly sloping but this is not obvious because of tightly curled tail.

Tail: Medium length, curled tightly over rump-loin area; long hair of tail mixes indistinguishably with similar hair of rump so that tail does not appear separate.

Colour: Acceptable colours black, rusty-black, white and various shades or grey and apricot.

Hindquarters: Strong and well muscled. Pelvis forming an angle of 90 degrees with thighbone. Well bent stifle. Hocks set fairly low. Wide pelvis desirable, especially in bitches.

Feet: Short, round, tight. Hindfeet slightly longer than forefeet. Nails strong, black or slate grey. Pads springy, dark grey in colour.

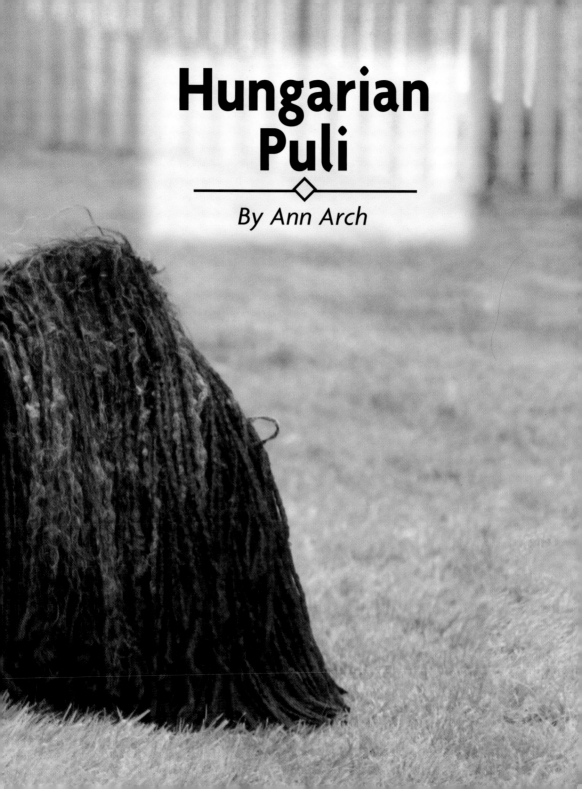

Hungarian Puli

◇

By Ann Arch

Contents

Hungarian Puli

PUBLISHED IN THE UNITED KINGDOM BY:

INTERPET
PUBLISHING
Vincent Lane, Dorking Surrey RH4 3YX England

ISBN 1-903098-52-1

PHOTO CREDITS:
Photos by Michael Trafford, with additional photos provided by:
Norvia Behling, TJ Calhoun, Carolina Biological Society,
Alex Davis, Doskocil, Isabelle Français, James Hayden-Yoav,
James R Hayden, RBP, Bill Jonas, Carol Ann Johnson,
Dwight R Kuhn, Dr Dennis Kunkel, Mikki Pet Products,
Phototake, Jean Claude Revy, Dr Andrew Spielman.
Illustrations by Renée Low.

Pulik are seen in black, rusty-black, white and various shades of grey and apricot, but not all countries accept all colours. Whatever the colour, it should be solid.

The background of the Puli is certainly lengthy and quite romantic. Although we regard the breed of Hungarian background, research indicates origins further east. When one compares the Puli with the Tibetan Terrier, for example, there are strong similarities. Moreover, the Tibetan breeds were not separated into varieties until about seventy years ago.

Research indicates the existence of Pulik as far back as the ninth century, in the region between the Don and Dnieper Rivers. However, even earlier, when sites of ancient civilisations were excavated, remains very much resembling the Puli were found. These date back as far as 2500 BC. At Eridu, on the Euphrates River, where excavation revealed one of the oldest cities on earth, archaeologists found the tomb of an eight-year-old princess named Il-De. She was buried with many of her possessions, among which was a tiny five-inch-tall alabaster statue of her little dog—clearly recognisable as a Puli! Believed to be around 6000 years old, the statue was last recorded as being exhibited in the National Museum of Iraq in Baghdad.

Although associated with Hungary, the Puli's origin can be traced further east. Similarities between the Puli and the Tibetan Terrier, shown here, are evident.

Tribes of nomadic horsemen who ranged across Asia had been known to the ancient Chinese since around 1200 BC. They called them the Puli Hou or the Destroyer Hun. Travelling further toward the west, by the fifth century AD, they had spread as far as Europe, by way of the Danube River. These invaders rode with their herds and their unruly semi-wild dogs. In AD 453, after their leader Attila died, they retreated to Asia.

Hungary had experienced other invaders, and in AD 567 came the Avars who eventually divided into tribes. One of the groups settled down and merged with the tribes of Northern India while others moved on beyond the Aral Sea and invaded the Carpathian Basin through the Danube. They were called White Hun, as well as Avar, and were thought to know the term 'Puli.' The word 'puli,' which commonly refers to a drover, can still be heard in parts of India, and other areas through which the Avars travelled. The Magyars lived for quite a while in the

Don and Dnieper River basins where these nomadic horsemen adapted to hunting, fishing and trading. In time, they gradually spread into Transylvania, over the Carpathian Mountains, where they were recorded around AD 895 or 896. They took with them large herds of cattle and flocks of sheep. The sheep, related to the Ovis Ammon Polh, were known as Argali. This horned breed spread as far as Bokhara and into China. Longhaired sheepskins dating back to 500 and 400 BC were found in the frozen wastelands of the Altai region.

The Magyars were a wild, hardy and rather fierce people who effectively drove out the earlier inhabitants of the wide Danube Valley where they then settled with their Pulik. Although the Puli was in Hungary by AD 899, there remained very similar dogs in the northern Himalayas.

Through the years, attacks were made by invaders on the settling Magyars, with the most serious onslaught by the Mongols, under Genghis Khan, in the thirteenth century. Having been successful over most of Asia, they tried to conquer parts of Europe, too. To them, the term 'puli' or 'buri' meant 'destroyer.'

Dogs similar to the Briard, shown here, were brought into Hungary for herding purposes and it is logical that interbreeding took place among these dogs and the Puli.

The native Hungarian population was quite depleted, and Germans later settled where the worst battles had taken place.

Inevitably, other animals were brought into Hungary, including Merino sheep and some herding dogs similar to the French Briard and Beauceron. In relief carvings of the twelfth and fourteenth centuries, varying types of dogs were depicted. Some had prick ears and curled tails while others had no tails and dropped ears.

Although the earliest verifiable recording of a Puli occurred in 1751 in a description of various hunting dogs, the Hungarians called the Puli and Pumi 'Juhasz-Kutyak'

In Hungary, the Pumi, shown here, and the Puli were both referred to as 'Juhasz-Kutyak,' meaning 'shepherds' dogs.'

THE PLURAL OF PULI
In Hungary, the plural of Puli is 'Pulix,' while in English-speaking countries the plural is 'Pulik,' though 'Pulis' is also used.

(Shepherds' Dogs). The Puli, as we know it today, came about by breeding to French and German shepherding breeds. In 1815, the Puli and the Pumi were scientifically classified as *Canis Familiaris Pomeranius*. In 1901 the Puli was renamed *Canis Familiaris Domesticus Hungaricus*. It was around that period that many countries decided to ensure the preservation of their native breeds. In the twentieth century, with the separation of the Puli and Pumi, sometimes an odd pup or two in a Puli litter can resemble a Pumi or even a Mudi, another similar herding dog, showing the comparatively recent split. In the beginning of the twentieth century, judges at dog shows were so uncertain of what they were seeking as the ideal at exhibitions that sometimes completely differing types were awarded prizes—prick-ears, short coats or pointed heads! Variations in size were also quite common in the first 30 or 40 years, as the early breed standard spoke of the Puli as 'a medium-sized sheepdog.' Prior to the Second World War, pictures showed the breed with quite long legs, coats often not in the now-familiar cords, and with tails that were sometimes carried lower and not always over the back.

Though recorded in some detail as show dogs at early shows in Budapest, both the Puli and Pumi were termed as 'Juhasz-Kutyak.' To the shepherd, they were known as two distinct breeds and given their own titles. In his book *Working Dogs of the World* (1947), Clifford Hubbard (affectionately known to all canine enthusiasts in Britain as 'Doggy Hubbard') noted that the Puli was starting to become quite well known outside of Hungary. Before the Second World War, Pulik were being bred in Austria, Germany and Italy, and American fanciers began to take an interest in the breed. The Puli was officially recognised by the American Kennel Club in May 1937. They had been introduced into the country in 1936, when the Maryland Agriculture Department used six Pulik among the breeds they tested for depth of intelligence of herding ability. Whereas all the working farm dogs were able to remember and act upon only 16 commands, the Puli outshone them all with a total of 75!

In Hungary, the organisation

The Beauceron is a French shepherd dog and cattle herder that many believe was used in the development of the Puli in Hungary.

formed to safeguard their sheepdog breeds had a very long name and became known by its initials: MEOE. Set up in 1899, the MEOE kept all early records of breeding and standards for the breeds encompassed. The veterinary surgeon attached to the Budapest Zoo, Dr Emil Raitsits, was influential in many ways, and the first Puli breed standard was eventually published in 1915. It was improved in 1924, when it was accepted by the Fédération Cynologique Internationale (FCI), which is the 'umbrella' organisation to which the majority of European countries belonged. The FCI has extended its area of operation now to many countries around the world. Dr Raitsits formed an alternative club in the early

PUMI

Another herding dog of Hungary that derives from the Puli is called the Pumi. This medium sized dog possesses unique upright ears and a curly coat, which, although long and thick, does not have a tendency to cord. The Pumi is a cattle drover and excels as a watchdog. In Hungary, the Pumi is the dog seen around town, while the Puli is seen more in the country and plains.

They were also prepared to accept for registration dogs that resembled the breed but had no paperwork to prove their origins. This confused not only the Hungarians but also people from other countries who, in good faith, purchased stock intended as foundation for setting up the breed overseas.

Following the Second World War, with the gene pool drastically reduced, showing and breeding resumed with quite strong jurisdiction over breeders by the MEOE. This organisation was responsible for the first shows and encouraged quality stock among breeders and exhibitors. As the level was so high, the show attracted enquiries from many countries, especially the USA and Britain. The British then exported stock to Australia and New Zealand.

The first mention of a Puli in England involved Clive of India, who was bartered from a German ex-serviceman by a Miss Turpin of Stafford for 20 Players cigarettes. He was shown at a Stafford Canine Society Show around 1950. The breed gained strength when the Ingus family lived in London for a while, before going on to America. In 1967 they arrived in London with their pet Puli Bodri. In 1969 they imported a bitch in whelp to the world-famous Int Ch Pusztai Furtos Ficko.

1930s but the FCI refused to recognise it. This club allowed for a variation in both size and colour (including particolours).

Hungarian Ch Kiscellehegyi Furge Csopi whelped four puppies in quarantine. As with all quarantine-born puppies, they were released as soon as they had been weaned, leaving their mother to complete her six months. At a show held by the Hammersmith Canine Society in 1970, Mr Ingus showed Bodri, and his floor-length corded coat attracted a great deal of attention. He and the puppies were subsequently featured in the national press and on television, where they aroused even more interest in this unusual breed. The Ingus family then moved to the USA in 1971.

Of the four puppies, one went to Pat Lanz, already very well known for her Rottweilers, under her 'Borgvaale' affix. A dog named Immerzu went to Mr & Mrs Terry Horan who later immigrated to Canada, while the remaining dog and bitch went to Nancy and Mike Tomlin who had pioneered the French Briard in the British show rings. Later, imports were brought in by Mrs Lanz and by Mrs Frou Stretton who had become interested in the Puli while her husband was working in Germany. Mrs Stretton's linguistic ability facilitated her dealings with the Hungarian breeders.

In America, following the Maryland experiment, a couple of Pulik were registered in 1937.

CORDED COATS

The Puli is not unique in the world of dogs for its cords. Corded coats occur on other purebred dogs including the Komondor (above), a giant white Hungarian guard dog. The Italian equivalent to the Puli is the Bergamasco (below), a corded herder that comes in shades of grey, black, and tan. Perhaps the most popular dog in the world that may be seen in cords is the Poodle, though this coat fashion has a very small following in the dog world today.

The Mudi is a herding dog similar to the Puli and Pumi; it is said that an occasional Puli pup can resemble a Mudi.

Perhaps the best remembered pre-war breeder was Mrs Sylvia Owen, whose breeding enjoyed success in the show ring, and from whom, many years later, Mrs Lanz imported the influential male Skysyl Watch Mt Big Stuff of Borgvaale (Willie). Later on, Mrs Lanz was to export a superb bitch sired by Willie back to Mrs Owen's Borgvaale Fruska's Ruby Ring, who was handled by a young lady called Ann Bowley. The bitch excelled in competition, and then made her place in breed history, as a top-producing dam, with 24 champion offspring to her credit. Willie's litter brother, Skysyl Harvey J Wallbanger became an all-time top sire with 49 champion offspring. In earlier times, the Pulik were shown in the USA with both corded and brushed-out coats, but this latter style is no longer fashionable.

Characteristics of the
HUNGARIAN PULI

The Puli is a lively and extremely intelligent breed. The breed loves to be a part of family life and particularly resents being ignored or only being included 'when convenient.' The dog will live quite happily both as a single dog and, providing that integration is carefully effected, will also be content as one of several. As a breed that was worked all the time, it has the stamina to perform its duties around the clock, every single day, so it is not really suited to a dull routine without exercise or other activity. As a family dog, it is ideal, always willing to play with the children. The Puli has the added value of acting as an effective warning instrument if strangers approach as it has excellent hearing. Again, they thoroughly enjoy participating in family activities, particularly whole days out with walking and romping about. We find that ours love to do some simple basic obedience—going to 'fetch' being the earliest. A favourite for such retrieves is a 'ragger,' which is just a short length of hard-wearing rope that is knotted at both ends. When Pulik compete seriously in obedience competition, they require a much smaller dumbbell than the normal size. Pulik have competed with success in obedience and agility, and in America they now frequently compete with other breeds in herding trials.

Perhaps the one thing that sets the breed apart and makes it so special is its coat. The Puli is born with a smooth and quite dense covering. This jacket soon starts to grow and will continue to grow

Pulik are extremely intelligent and playful dogs.

longer and longer throughout their entire life. Quite tough in their constitution, Pulik are easy to feed, not requiring exotic or high-protein meals. After all, they would have had little chance to enjoy the high protein in meat, as they were living with nomad shepherds, and making do with whatever scraps were thrown to them. The Puli is a wiry, fine-boned dog. Any extra weight would only slow down the animal and, in time, put a strain on its heart and lungs. It is the easiest breed we have ever owned, not only for its general health but also for house-training. As long as a regular routine is established early, they are soon trustworthy around the house.

The Puli is a true family dog...he loves to be part of his owners' lives, he adapts well to most any living situation and he fares equally well in a single- or multi-dog household.

Its unusual coat needs particular attention if it is to be maintained in good condition. For example, the Puli should never be left outdoors in all weathers. If the dog is to be put outdoors in a run, a portion should be covered to prevent rain soaking the dog's coat as it will take quite a while to dry. If left wet, it can soon become smelly and offensive to all!

What type of home is best? Pulik adapt to wherever their families live. Flat-dwellers can cope very well with the breed as long as they follow a regular exercise routine.

From the time that the Puli arrives in its new home, you must remember that you have an ultra-intelligent animal living with you. There is an old saying, 'A Puli is not a dog. A Puli is a Puli.' This sums up their distinctive character very well! They are very much like active and intelligent children who respond well to sensible discipline. As long as they learn what is expected of them as soon as possible, they soon become well-behaved members of the household. From the time they arrive and become accustomed to their new surroundings, it takes a very short time for them to adjust to your routine.

Feeding and exercising should be carried out at regular times, which helps them to develop a sense of security. It is also important that if they are to be taken out and about in a car, they should begin with some preliminary short trips. Early forays may cause a little car-sickness, or they

may be tempted to start jumping around. For this reason, we definitely recommend a travel box or wire crate. Such a device not only will keep them secure but also will be regarded as their home.

In these important early weeks, you will decide just which parts of the house are forbidden to them, so that they quickly become accustomed to their limits. Our dogs, as part of the family unit, have never been forbidden any access. However, should anyone visit who is not dog-minded, then I only have to say 'crates' and they will go to their crates and stand ready to enter. Of course, there is always the reward of a biscuit when they are securely inside. The area in which their crates are kept should be a comfortable cool temperature and quiet.

The corded Puli jacket is quite distinctive and their owners are delighted to have such an attractive, unique breed. However, there

The Puli is one of the few corded breeds in dogdom; this type of coat is very distinctive and requires maintenance. If coat care is a burden for the pet owner, the coat can be trimmed shorter.

may be circumstances when it is impossible to maintain such a coat. Then they can be clipped down, or perhaps the cords reduced to around 6–7.5 cms. Keeping the mature jacket in full show condition is quite an undertaking, and those with several Pulik to cope with will often clip the coats on those that are no longer being exhibited. It is far better that you keep the Puli clean and sweet-smelling rather than retain a long coat that is untended and dirty. The coat is Nature's own insulation, being capable of keeping the animal

Originally bred as herding dogs with the stamina to work all day, the Puli is a very active dog with superior intelligence. He needs activity and will welcome off-lead exercise and retrieving games with his owners.

This is why people have dogs as pets...the dog/owner bond is priceless.

warm and dry, and stopping the sun from reaching and burning the skin. In the warmer weather, we clip off the coat under the belly, from behind the elbow, right along the rib cage, belly, and on to the inside of the top of the hindlegs. When it's warm, they tend to sleep on their backs so that they stay cooler.

Caring breeders will only breed from stock that has been screened under official schemes for any known hereditary problems. People may be concerned at the mention of such problems for there are known to be about 300 identified hereditary problems in the dog world, but the number of currently identified hereditary defects in the human world is over 1000! This surely puts it into perspective. In the Puli it is customary to have hips x-rayed, which is done in most breeds. The radiographic check is done at around 13 to 18 months of age. Countries will all have their own schemes and differing levels of evaluation. In the UK, these are called hip scores. The perfect score is 0/0, while highest is a total of the two sides of 106. Each hip, on the x-ray plate, is carefully measured, with a maximum of 53 for each side. These are then added together. The mean average score for the Puli in the UK is around 19. Although the condition has been known in many types of animals for centuries, awareness of it in the dog population has only come about within the past 50 years.

Anyone contemplating breeding should have their bitch's eyes declared clear and should use a stud dog that has also acceptable eye status. Resulting puppies should be eye screened as a whole litter prior to dispersal to their new homes. This is best done at seven to eight weeks of age. Any conscientious breeder will willingly produce copies of hip and eye status for prospective puppy purchasers.

Keeping your Puli clean, comfortable and healthy is not difficult, and you should learn early on what is required, before your bring your Puli home.

The Breed Standard for the
HUNGARIAN PULI

Any breed of animal that is to be exhibited needs to have a description of an ideal by which it is to be judged. The blueprint of the perfect specimen, by which a judge evaluates those before him, is called a breed standard. Most kennel clubs will adopt a standard that is based on that of the country of origin, but there will sometimes be slight variations on some small aspects. If anyone is to judge overseas, then he will need to be aware of the published standard of the country concerned.

In Britain, The Kennel Club has grouped the breeds into seven groups, and the Puli is included in the Pastoral Group, formerly a part of the Working Group. The Pastoral Group, as the title suggests, covers the farmers' and shepherds' dogs. As with the majority of the Pastoral breeds, the first impression of the Puli is of a good weatherproof coat on a strong, functional animal. However, in common with most other breeds, the number being exhibited all over the world far outnumbers those being used for their original purposes. Despite the greater emphasis on exhibition, all breeds should still be quite capable of doing the job for which they were developed. This means that a judge should be aware of correct balance and construction beneath the coat. In more recent years, perhaps greater emphasis has been placed upon coats and theatrical handling than might be good for any breed. It is a sad day for any breed attributed with working ability, if any type of exaggerated presentation is considered to be of greater importance than the quality of the dog underneath. Coats may come and go, according to the season of the year, but the construction underneath remains!

We will be discussing the breed standard for the Hungarian Puli as adopted by The Kennel Club, the author's comments being in *italics*.

THE KENNEL CLUB STANDARD FOR THE HUNGARIAN PULI

General Appearance: Sturdy, muscular, wiry, with fine bone. Whole well covered with long (according to age), profuse corded coat. Long hair overshadows eyes like an umbrella. Viewed from side, trunk and limbs should present square figure.

It's quite a surprise, on first handling a Puli, to find under the enormous mature corded coat, a

The quality of a Puli for show purposes is evaluated according to the official breed standard. Different countries have slightly different standards; therefore, there is some variation from country to country.

That they are wary of strangers is indicated by an unwillingness to launch themselves on visitors. We always advise anyone unknown to our dogs that he should start off by ignoring them. In a short time, an inquisitive little Hungarian will approach them as Pulik are certainly curious.

lean, hard, conditioned, fine-boned and very wiry little animal. When observed from the side, if you visualise the body and limbs minus the neck and head, they should be approximate to a square.

Characteristics: Herding dog, medium-sized, nimble and extremely intelligent.

Perhaps 'medium-sized' is a little misleading, for top height is given at 44 cms (17.5 ins) for males and 41 cms (16 ins) for females. Oversize is not desirable as it can lead to coarseness.

Temperament: Lively, wary of strangers, but not displaying nervousness or unprovoked aggression.

Head and Skull: Disregarding hair, head small and fine with slightly domed skull. From front it appears round, from side almost elliptical. Muzzle one-third length of head, with well defined stop, not snipey but bluntly rounded. Arches of eye socket well defined, nose relatively large and black, eye rims and flews black in all colours.

The head of the Puli is very special. Under no circumstances should judges ignore the call for correct size, proportions and fineness, coupled with the domed skull. The skull-muzzle rations of two-thirds to one-third is of great importance, for a too lengthy muzzle immediately suggests coarseness. The lack of dome on the skull will also lead to an impression of coarseness. The need for a relatively large nose is understandable in any working animal that needs to produce a turn of speed or enduring gait, when they will require unimpeded inhalation of air quickly into the lungs.

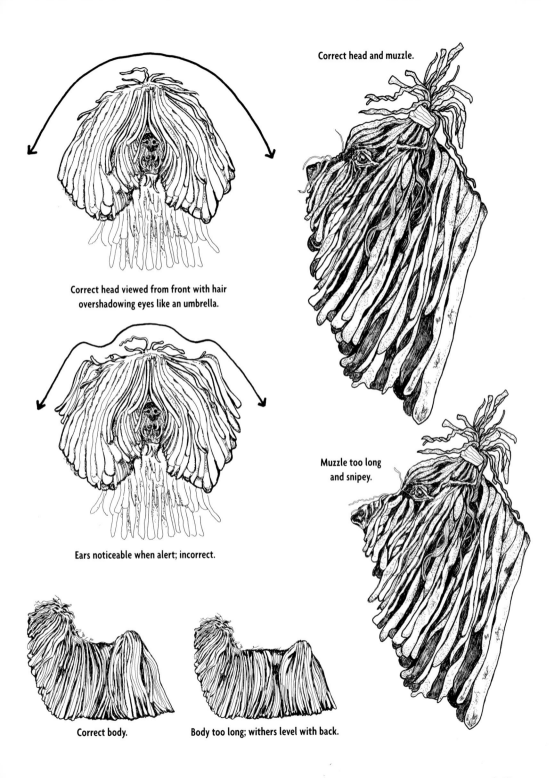

Correct head viewed from front with hair overshadowing eyes like an umbrella.

Correct head and muzzle.

Ears noticeable when alert; incorrect.

Muzzle too long and snipey.

Correct body.

Body too long; withers level with back.

Medium-sized, dark brown eyes with a lively expression are typical in all coat colours, according to the standard.

Eyes: Medium size, dark brown with lively expression.

The description should apply to all colours, and eye rims should always be well pigmented. In a dog that will be out working at times in intense sunlight, lack of pigment could allow the skin to become burnt.

Ears: Set slightly below level of skull, V-shaped, pendant, of medium size, covered with long hair. Length of ears about half length of head. Ears do not appear noticeable, even when alert.

This is very descriptive.

Mouth: Roof uniformly dark or variegated with deep pigmented spots on dark base. Flews tight and black. Tongue bright red. Jaws and teeth strong with perfect scissor bite, i.e. upper teeth closely overlapping lower teeth and set square to the jaws.

Again, the description is so good.

Neck: Set at an angle of 45 degrees to horizontal, of medium length, tight skinned and muscular. When fully coated, neck appears to merge with body.

There can be no doubt as to the requirement. Perhaps some judges may be influenced into believing that a longer neck is better—some have even gone as far as to praise a 'good reachy neck'—but that is quite incorrect. The top of the head, when viewed from the side, is only a little higher than the top arch of the tail, giving a balanced appearance.

Forequarters: Shoulders well laid. Elbows tight. Forelegs straight and muscular, and viewed from any angle, vertical.

A real understanding of the dog and its working needs is essential in order to fully appreciate correct forehand construction. The brief reference to the shoulder, in my opinion, is inadequate. A good shoulder is essential in an animal that must be capable of bursts of strong and agile action. Working animals, dealing with quick-witted and cunning farm animals, must have the strength and ability to turn quickly. Without correct angulation, and the balance of the two main bones that make up the shoulder, clean forward reach and the ability to maintain untiring action are impeded if unbalanced. Most breeds will have a reasonable length and angulation of the bone that goes back from the forechest and up to the withers (scapula). However, a fairly common fault in so many breeds can be shortness or lack of angulation of what is called the 'upper arm' (the bone that goes from the forechest, back down to the elbow). If there is a lack of angulation in the shoulder, then the animal will be restricted in the length of forward reach it can attain. In turn, this will require a lot of tiny steps to cover a length of ground. An animal with better angulation will not need to take so many steps to cover the same distance, resulting in a less tired dog. Elbows should fit in neatly under the rib cage, and not be loose. This ensures strong and quite straight action when viewed from the front, without too much width between the legs.

Body: Withers slightly higher than level of back, which is of medium length. Loin short and broad,

belly slightly tucked up. Ribs deep, rib cage broadening from behind elbows and well sprung. Rump short and slightly sloping but this is not obvious because of tightly curled tail.

This is described very well, and due to the very large coat in the mature Puli the body must be checked carefully by a 'hands-on' examination.

Hindquarters: Strong and well muscled. Pelvis forming an angle of 90 degrees with thighbone. Well bent stifle. Hocks set fairly low. When viewed from the rear, the legs should be parallel, with feet turning neither in nor out. Wide pelvis desirable, especially in bitches.

Again, this is a good description, and compares well to the need for forehand angulation. The standard mentions fairly low set

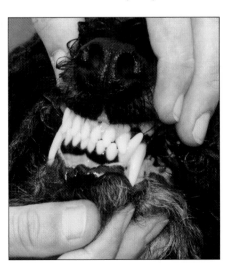

Jaws of the Puli must be strong, with the teeth in a perfect scissor bite as shown.

hocks and the actual joint should be checked for strength to ensure that there is no sub-luxation (sloping forward, rather like a double joint).

Feet: Short, round, tight. Hindfeet slightly longer than forefeet. Nails strong, black or slate grey. Pads springy, dark grey in colour.

This very important part of the dog should be checked carefully, for if the dog is to do a day's work, it is essential that feet should not be spread or have thin pads.

Tail: Medium length, curled tightly over rump-loin area; long hair of tail mixes indistinguishably with similar hair of rump so that tail does not appear separate.

In some youngsters, when excited, the tail may be held a fraction loose. This can also indicate a degree of apprehension when the dogs first enter the show ring. In mature dogs, the tail should be carried firmly.

Correct tail. Incorrect tail; it should not appear separate from rump. Incorrect tail set; too low.

Gait/Movement: Stride not far-reaching. Gallop short. Typical movement short-stepping, very quick, in harmony with lively disposition. Movement never heavy, lethargic or lumbering.

All too often there is confusion over interpretation of this section of the standard. The Puli must have the capability for quick and sudden turns when required, and this would be impossible if the dog were to lack shoulder and hind angulation. The movement should have a light spring to it, and that is brought about by what can best be compared to the suspension of a car. If you don't have good suspension in your car, then every bump or uneven surface over which you travel will result in shock waves travelling upwards. In a car, the passengers soon become uncomfortable; in similar fashion, the dog would soon become tired. Moreover, it is likely that in order to get quickly around to the other side of a flock, the Puli will spring up and run over the backs of sheep. This would be a struggle, if not impossible, if the angulations were lacking, thus preventing the agile, light, upward spring.

Coat: Correct proportion of top and undercoat creates, naturally, the desired cords. Matting and felting to be avoided, and a combed coat is as undesirable as a neglected one. Coat generally longest on hindquarters, shortest on head and feet. Some dogs will grow a floor-length coat.

There are various accepted coat colours in the Puli. Some colours may have black or white hairs intermingled, but the importance is the overall appearance of a solid colour.

Although all Pulik may look alike to the casual viewer, there is variety in the coat types that are possible. We once had a litter of four, all ending up with different types of cords in maturity. You may have the fine, rounded cord, the thicker and not-so-tight but still rounded cord, the flat 'ribbon' type that can be quite hard or perhaps slightly softer and loose in its composition, or the occasional cord that appears to be composed of both felt and a little softer texture, which are usually slower in forming. Whatever type of cord starts to form, it is inadvisable to attempt to change it.

Colour: Acceptable colours black, rusty-black, white and various shades or grey and apricot. Black sometimes appears weathered, rusty, or with slight intermingling of white hairs. Grey and apricot in all their shades may have an intermingling of black or white hairs, with or without black mask, ear tips and tail tip. The overall appearance of all variants must be that of a solid colour. A white spot on chest of not more than 5 cms (2 ins) is permissible. A few white hairs on feet also permissible. Body skin should be well pigmented and slate grey in colour, especially in blacks and greys.

According to the standards of some countries, not all colours are acceptable. In the UK, we accept black, white and shades of grey and apricot, but their interpretation is sometimes rather loose.

*Having seen and judged geneti-
cally pure whites, it is quite
impressive to observe their solid
black pigment on nose, eye rims,
flews, pads, nails and all with
quite a good slate-coloured skin.
Some that are registered as
'white' can in later life be seen to
have lost the important pigmentation and this would be severely
penalised by judges in FCI
countries. The foregoing remarks
also apply to some which have
classed as apricot. The country of
origin has never altered its
pigment requirements.
Recognised in some places is the
coloration 'Facko.' This is
likened to an intermingling of
grey and apricot, and will carry
good pigmentation. Our original
bitch was born and first
registered as grey, but before she
was old enough to exhibit, she
turned apricot and her registration details were altered. As a
black-masked apricot, with
excellent pigment, she became
the UK's first (and only) apricot
champion. However, in later life,
as a Veteran, the growth of grey
coat could not be ignored, and
we believe that she could have
been termed 'Facko.' As it was,
she produced some very good
grey and started off a line that
still favours that colour.*

Size: Height: dogs: 40–44 cms
(16–17.5 ins); bitches: 37–41 cms
(14.5–16 ins).

Weight: dogs: 13–15 kgs (28.5–33
lbs); bitches: 10–13 kgs (22–28.5 lbs).

*As a judge, when seeking
breed type balance and
soundness, it can be difficult to
make decisions that are
understood by all. In Britain, we
don't have disqualifications, only
the need to take faults in proportion to the dog as a whole, which
allows one to put up an animal
that might be fractionally under
or over the ideal sizes, providing
that it has sufficient other
qualities. Type and balance are
so important, and it does seem
hard to totally penalise on one
specific point, and be forced to
place favourably an animal
which is within the sizes, but
lacks breed type or balance. The
word 'type' is frequently used,
but is far from easy to describe.
My own interpretation is that
'type' is what makes a breed
special, and identifiable, apart
from others with similarities. If
we didn't have 'breed type' then
all similar breeds could eventually end up very much alike.*

Faults: Any departure from the
foregoing points should be
considered a fault and the
seriousness with which the fault
should be regarded in exact
proportion to its degree.

Note: Male animals should have
apparently normal testicles fully
descended into the scrotum.

CHOOSING AND REARING YOUR PULI PUPPY

As breeders, we have always found newborn Puli puppies to be really very contented little dears. We always think that they are rather like fat little slugs at the beginning. All they want is to feed and sleep. However, the time comes when they start to move around and develop personalities. We think Puli babies are born intelligent, compared to other breeds we have owned. At birth, one of ours, even before being expelled from its mother, was reaching round and trying to suckle. As soon as they are able, they'll start to crawl around with quite amazing determination. Even the opening of the eyes seems to be very early. Most Puli pups are quite inquisitive and bold, so the choice of pup can not be decided by which is the outgoing character. Depending on whether you wish to show your Puli, or keep it as a pet, it is perhaps better to be guided by the breeder, or take along an experienced friend as the task of choosing is not easy. One would expect a price difference between the one that appears to be a show prospect and another

that may have some point that would make it not quite so desirable for exhibition. If perhaps a pup has a noticeable flash of white, which will probably not disappear as the puppy grows, that Puli will probably make a super family pet. We have found that to scrutinize puppies in the first 36 to 48 hours following birth, it was possible to assess bone and body proportions, overall balance and construction, before the well-fed puppy started to gain weight.

Caring breeders will have bred from a fit and healthy bitch and will do everything possible to ensure that the litter thrives. Sensible pre-natal feeding of the mother will continue after she whelps so that all possible

BOY OR GIRL?

An important consideration to be discussed is the sex of your puppy. For a family companion, a bitch may be the better choice, considering the female's inbred concern for all young creatures and her accompanying tolerance and patience. It is always advisable to spay a pet bitch, which may guarantee her a longer life.

PREPARING FOR PUP

Unfortunately, when a puppy is bought by someone who does not take into consideration the time and attention that dog ownership requires, it is the puppy who suffers when he is either abandoned or placed in a shelter by a frustrated owner. So all of the 'homework' you do in preparation for your pup's arrival will benefit you both. The more informed you are, the more you will know what to expect and the better equipped you will be to handle the ups and downs of raising a puppy. Hopefully, everyone in the household is willing to do his part in raising and caring for the pup. The anticipation of owning a dog often brings a lot of promises from excited family members: 'I will walk him every day,' 'I will feed him,' 'I will housebreak him,' etc., but these things take time and effort, and promises can easily be forgotten once the novelty of the new pet has worn off.

goodness passes through her milk into the whelps. As soon as they are ready for weaning, we have found that the most forward of our pups will attempt to join mum at her food dish. The youngsters will gradually go on to suitable, quality nutrition, so that by the time you collect you new pup it will have received the best possible care. Breeders will also have wormed the litter prior to your collecting your addition.

Before the important collection day arrives, you will have made enquiries as to what foods you should have ready, also food dish, water bowl, etc. Don't spend a great deal of money on a tiny bed, as puppies grow quite fast and by the time you have an adult in its full coat, it will certainly need something larger than it did at eight weeks of age. We advise that if owners want to get a dog bed, then they start off with the full-sized one, but that they can put a smaller, shallow cardboard box inside so that the puppy has something cosy to curl up in.

ARE YOU A FIT OWNER?

If the breeder from whom you are buying a puppy asks you a lot of personal questions, do not be insulted. Such a breeder wants to be sure that you will be a fit provider for his puppy.

Breeders normally wean puppies on to five meals a day, starting off with milk/cereals, and then adding a little scraped beef that will in time be replaced with minced beef. We alternate with milk and meat to start and then turn the breakfast into milk and cereal, lunch of meat, tea of milk and supper of meat. If a puppy goes to bed on a comfortably full stomach, it is more likely to sleep well. The next feed to eliminate was tea, making three meals a day by the time that the pups were ready to go to new homes. As we reduced the number of feeds, the amounts given were gradually increased. When the pups indicated that they were ready, we cut out the mid-day meal, leaving just breakfast and supper. As the last meal was gradually increased in quantity, so we made the breakfast more of a drink than a proper meal. By

YOUR SCHEDULE . . .

If you lead an erratic, unpredictable life, with daily or weekly changes in your work requirements, consider the problems of owning a puppy. The new puppy has to be fed regularly, socialised (loved, petted, handled, introduced to other people) and, most importantly, allowed to visit outdoors for toilet training. As the dog gets older, it can be more tolerant of deviations in its feeding and toilet relief.

DO YOUR HOMEWORK!

In order to know whether or not a puppy will fit into your lifestyle, you need to assess his personality. A good way to do this is to interact with his parents. Your pup inherits not only his appearance but also his personality and temperament from the sire and dam. If the parents are fearful or overly aggressive, these same traits may likely show up in your puppy.

this time the puppy will almost be 12 months of age. There can be no firm time given for meal changes, as puppies will vary in their needs, even among littermates. Our experience with the Puli puppy is that it displays very adult tastes and does not tolerate baby feeding for long.

Do keep in touch with your breeder for he will care about the welfare and the future of the puppies he has so carefully reared and will be eager to learn of your progress. He will be the best source of help and advice if you have queries or problems. The caring breeder will have carefully evaluated you as a prospective owner, especially if you have no previous experience. Be understanding as to his concern over the puppy's future

PUPPY SELECTION

Your selection of a good puppy can be determined by your needs. A show potential or a good pet? It is your choice. Every puppy, however, should be of good temperament. Although show-quality puppies are bred and raised with emphasis on physical conformation, responsible breeders strive for equally good temperament. Do not buy from a breeder who concentrates solely on physical beauty at the expense of personality.

'YOU BETTER SHOP AROUND!'

Finding a reputable breeder that sells healthy pups is very important, but make sure that the breeder you choose is not only someone you respect but also with whom you feel comfortable. Your breeder will be a resource long after you buy your puppy, and you must be able to call with reasonable questions without being made to feel like a pest! If you don't connect on a personal level, investigate some other breeders before making a final decision.

and don't be upset when he expects you to give certain undertakings. A most important part of modern changes in ownership is frequently the call for parties to sign a form of sales agreement (contract). You should not be surprised to be asked to agree that if for any reason you are unable to keep the puppy you will ensure that the breeder is the first to know, and be given the opportunity of either taking it back or being involved in its re-homing. We should all feel responsible for anything that we breed, from the day it is born until the day it dies. Some breeds have a rescue or welfare section, but this service should only be called upon for help in times of emergency, illness or other sad circumstances.

INSURANCE

Many good breeders will offer you insurance with your new puppy, which is an excellent idea. The first few weeks of insurance will probably be covered free of charge or with only minimal cost, allowing you to take up the policy when this expires. If you own a pet dog, it is sensible to take out such a policy as veterinary fees can be high, although routine vaccinations and boosters are not covered. Look carefully at the many options open to you before deciding which suits you best.

PREPARING PUPPY'S PLACE IN YOUR HOME

Much as you would prepare a nursery for a newborn baby, you will need to designate a place in your home that will be the puppy's own. How you prepare your home will depend on how much freedom the dog will be allowed. Whatever you decide, you must ensure that he has a place that he can 'call his own.'

When you bring your new puppy into your home, you are bringing him into what will become his home as well. Obviously, you did not buy a puppy so that he could take over your house, but in order for a puppy to grow into a stable, well-adjusted dog, he has to feel comfortable in his surroundings. Remember, he is leaving the

PUPPY APPEARANCE

Your puppy should have a well-fed appearance but not a distended abdomen, which may indicate worms or incorrect feeding, or both. The body should be firm, with a solid feel. The skin of the abdomen should be pale pink and clean, without signs of scratching or rash. Check the hind legs to make certain that dewclaws were removed, if any were present at birth.

You should have acquired a crate BEFORE you brought your new Puli puppy home. The crate will be your best friend as well as your puppy's.

warmth and security of his mother and littermates, as well as the familiarity of the only place he has ever known, so it is important to make his transition as easy as possible. By preparing a place in your home for the puppy, you are making him feel as welcome as possible in a strange new place. It should not take him long to get used to it, but the sudden shock of being transplanted is somewhat traumatic for a young pup. Imagine how a small child would feel in the same situation—that is how your puppy must be feeling. It is up

HOW VACCINES WORK

If you've just bought a puppy, you surely know the importance of having your pup vaccinated, but do you understand how vaccines work? Vaccines contain the same bacteria or viruses that cause the disease you want to prevent, but they have been chemically modified so that they don't cause any harm. Instead, the vaccine causes your dog to produce antibodies that fight the harmful bacteria. Thus, if your pup is exposed to the disease in the future, the antibodies will destroy the viruses or bacteria.

preferred tools for show puppies as well as pet puppies. Crates are not cruel—crates have many humane and highly effective uses in dog care and training. For example, crate training is a very popular and very successful

DID YOU KNOW?
You should not even think about buying a puppy that looks sick, undernourished, overly frightened or nervous. Sometimes a timid puppy will warm up to you after a 30-minute 'let's-get-acquainted' session

DID YOU KNOW?
Breeders rarely release puppies until they are eight to ten weeks of age. This is an acceptable age for most breeds of dog, excepting toy breeds, which are not released until around 12 weeks, given their petite sizes. If a breeder has a puppy that is 12 weeks or more, it is likely well socialised and housetrained. Be sure that it is otherwise healthy before deciding to take it home.

to you to reassure him and to let him know, 'Little chap, you are going to like it here!'

WHAT YOU SHOULD BUY

CRATE

To someone unfamiliar with the use of crates in dog training, it may seem like punishment to shut a dog in a crate, but this is not the case at all. Although all breeders do not advocate crate training, more and more breeders and trainers are recommending crates as

Your local pet shop will have a range of dog crates from which you can select the one which best suits your needs.

seek out the comfort and retreat of a den—you just happen to be providing him with something a little more luxurious than what his early ancestors enjoyed.

At our home, Puli babies are introduced to wire crates at an early age. There is always a crate around for the pup, with its door left open. They can walk in and out, curl up on the bedding, and accept it as part of their everyday surroundings. As it is always there, it holds no terror. We also find it helpful to feed the puppy inside the crate at times, so they only associate the crate with pleasure. When they have been playing and need a rest, settling in the crate is a welcome idea. Close the door and leave them quiet.

As far as purchasing a crate, the type that you buy is up to you. It will most likely be one of the two most popular types: wire or fibreglass. There are advantages and disadvantages to each type. For example, a wire crate is more open, allowing the air to flow through and affording the dog a view of what is going on around him while a fibreglass crate is sturdier. Both can double as travel crates, providing protection for the dog. The size of the crate is another thing to consider. Puppies do not stay puppies forever—in fact, sometimes it seems as if they grow right before your eyes. A

housebreaking method. A crate can keep your dog safe during travel and, perhaps most importantly, a crate provides your dog with a place of his own in your home. It serves as a 'doggie bedroom' of sorts—your Puli can curl up in his crate when he wants to sleep or when he just needs a break. Many dogs sleep in their crates overnight. With soft bedding and his favourite toy, a crate becomes a cosy pseudo-den for your dog. Like his ancestors, he too will

small-sized crate may be fine for a very young Puli pup, but it will not do him much good for long! Unless you have the money and the inclination to buy a new crate every time your pup has a growth spurt, it is better to get one that will accommodate your dog both as a pup and at full size. A medium-sized crate will be necessary for a full-grown Puli, who stands approximately 17.5 inches high.

BEDDING

Veterinary bedding in the dog's crate will help the dog feel more at home and you may also like to pop in a small blanket. This will take the place of the leaves, twigs, etc., that the pup would use in the wild to make a den; the pup can make his own 'burrow' in the crate. Although your pup is far removed from his den-making ancestors, the denning instinct is still a part of his genetic makeup. Second, until you take your pup home, he has been sleeping amidst the warmth of his mother and litter-mates, and while a blanket is not the same as a warm, breathing body, it still provides heat and something with which to snuggle. You will want to wash your pup's bedding frequently in case he has an accident in his crate, and replace or remove any blanket that becomes ragged and starts to fall apart.

CRATE TRAINING TIPS

During crate training, you should partition off the section of the crate in which the pup stays. If he is given too big an area, this will hinder your training efforts. Crate training is based on the fact that a dog does not like to soil his sleeping quarters, so it is ineffective to keep a pup in a crate that is so big that he can eliminate in one end and get far enough away from it to sleep. Also, you want to make the crate den-like for the pup. Blankets and a favourite toy will make the crate cosy for the small pup; as he grows, you may want to evict some of his 'roommates' to make more room.

It will take some coaxing at first, but be patient. Given some time to get used to it, your pup will adapt to his new home-within-a-home quite nicely.

TOYS, TOYS, TOYS!

With a big variety of dog toys available, and so many that look like they would be a lot of fun for a dog, be careful in your selection. It is amazing what a set of puppy teeth can do to an innocent-looking toy, so, obviously, safety is a major consideration. Be sure to choose the most durable products that you can find. Hard nylon bones and toys are a safe bet, and many of them are offered in different scents and flavours that will be sure to capture your dog's attention. It is always fun to play a game of catch with your dog, and there are balls and flying discs that are specially made to withstand dog teeth.

Toys

Toys are a must for dogs of all ages, especially for curious playful pups. Puppies are the 'children' of the dog world, and what child does not love toys? Chew toys provide enjoyment for both dog and owner—your dog will enjoy playing with his favourite toys, while you will enjoy the fact that they distract him from your expensive shoes and leather sofa. Puppies love to chew; in fact, chewing is a physical need for pups as they are teething, and everything looks appetising! The full range of your possessions—from old tea towel to Oriental carpet—are fair game in the eyes of a teething pup. Puppies are not all that discerning when it comes to finding something to literally 'sink their teeth into'— everything tastes great!

Puli puppies are fairly aggressive chewers and only the hardest, strongest toys should be offered to them. Breeders advise owners to resist stuffed toys, because they can become de-stuffed in no time. The overly excited pup may ingest the stuffing, which is neither digestible nor nutritious.

Similarly, squeaky toys are quite popular, but must be avoided for the Puli. Perhaps a squeaky toy can be used as an aid in training, but not for free play. If a pup 'disembowels' one of these, the small plastic squeaker inside can be dangerous if swallowed. Monitor the condition of all your pup's toys carefully and get rid of any that have been chewed to the point of becoming potentially dangerous.

Be careful of natural bones, which have a tendency to splinter into sharp, dangerous pieces. Also be careful of rawhide, which can turn into pieces that are easy to swallow and become a mushy mess on your carpet.

LEAD

A nylon lead is probably the best option as it is the most resistant to puppy teeth should your pup take a liking to chewing on his lead. Of course, this is a habit that should be nipped in the bud, but if your pup likes to chew on his lead he has a very slim chance of being able to chew through the strong nylon.

MENTAL AND DENTAL

Toys not only help your puppy get the physical and mental stimulation he needs but also provide a great way to keep his teeth clean. Hard rubber or nylon toys, especially those constructed with grooves, are designed to scrape away plaque, preventing bad breath and gum infection.

PLAY'S THE THING

Teaching the puppy to play with his toys in running and fetching games is an ideal way to help the puppy develop muscle, learn motor skills and bond with you his owner and master.

He also needs to learn how to inhibit his bite reflex and never to use his teeth on people, forbidden objects and other animals in play. Whenever you play with your puppy, you make the rules. This becomes an important message to your puppy in teaching him that you are the pack leader and control everything he does in life. Once your dog accepts you as his leader, your relationship with him will be cemented for life.

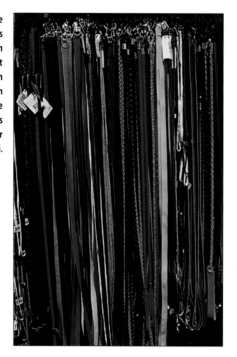

There are many leads available from your local pet store from which you can choose one that is suitable for your Puli.

Nylon leads are also lightweight, which is good for a young Puli who is just getting used to the idea of walking on a lead. For everyday walking and safety purposes, the nylon lead is a good choice. As your pup grows up and gets used to walking on the lead, you may want to purchase a flexible lead. These leads allow you to extend the length to give the dog a broader area to explore or to shorten the length to keep the dog near you. Of course there are special leads for training purposes, and specially made leather harnesses, but these are not necessary for routine walks.

COLLAR

Your pup should get used to wearing a collar all the time since you will want to attach his ID tags to it. You have to attach the lead to something! A lightweight nylon collar is a good choice; make sure that it fits snugly enough so that the pup cannot wriggle out of it, but is loose enough so that it will not be uncomfortably tight around the pup's neck. You should be able to fit a finger between the pup and the collar. It may take some time for your pup to get used to wearing the collar, but soon he will not even notice that it is there. Choke collars are made for training, but should only be used by an experienced handler.

FOOD AND WATER BOWLS

Your pup will need two bowls, one for food and one for water. You may want two sets of bowls, one for inside and one for outside, depending on where the dog will be fed and where he will be spending time. Stainless steel or sturdy plastic bowls are popular choices. Plastic bowls are more chewable. Dogs tend not to chew on the steel variety, which can be sterilised. It is important to buy sturdy bowls since anything is in danger of being chewed by puppy teeth and you do not want your dog to be constantly chewing apart his

CHOOSE AN APPROPRIATE COLLAR

The BUCKLE COLLAR is the standard collar used for everyday purpose. Be sure that you adjust the buckle on growing puppies. Check it every day. It can become too tight overnight! These collars can be made of leather or nylon. Attach your dog's identification tags to this collar.

The CHOKE COLLAR is the usual collar recommended for training. It is constructed of highly polished steel so that it slides easily through the stainless steel loop. The idea is that the dog controls the pressure around its neck and he will stop pulling if the collar becomes uncomfortable. Never leave a choke collar on your dog when not training.

The HALTER is for a trained dog that has to be restrained to prevent running away, chasing a cat and the like. Considered the most humane of all collars, it is frequently used on smaller dogs for which collars are not comfortable.

Dog bowls are made from a variety of materials: heavy plastic, pottery and stainless steel are popular choices.

PHOTO COURTESY OF MIKKI PET PRODUCTS.

bowl (for his safety and for your purse!).

CLEANING SUPPLIES

Until a pup is housetrained you will be doing a lot of cleaning. Accidents will occur, which is acceptable in the beginning because the puppy does not know any better. All you can do is be prepared to clean up any 'accidents.' Old rags, towels, newspapers and a safe disinfectant are good to have on hand.

BEYOND THE BASICS

The items previously discussed are the bare necessities. You will find out what else you need as you go along—grooming supplies, flea/tick protection, baby gates to partition a room, etc. These things will vary depending on your situation but it is important that you have everything you need to feed and make your Puli comfortable in his first few days at home.

NATURAL TOXINS

Examine your grass and garden landscaping before bringing your puppy home. Many varieties of plants have leaves, stems or flowers that are toxic if ingested, and you can depend on a curious puppy to investigate them. Ask your vet for information on poisonous plants or research them at your library.

PUPPY-PROOFING

Thoroughly puppy-proof your house before bringing your puppy home. Never use roach or rodent poisons in any area accessible to the puppy. Avoid the use of toilet cleaners. Most dogs are born with 'toilet sonar' and will take a drink if the lid is left open. Also keep the rubbish secured and out of reach.

It is necessary to clean up after your dog no matter where he relieves himself. You can purchase a device that will make the cleaning-up process less troublesome.

PUPPY-PROOFING YOUR HOME

Aside from making sure that your Puli will be comfortable in your home, you also have to make sure that your home is safe for your Puli. This means taking precautions that your pup will not get into anything he should not get into and that there is nothing within his reach that may harm him should he sniff it, chew it, inspect it, etc. This probably seems obvious since, while you are primarily concerned with your pup's safety, at the same time you do not want your belongings to be ruined. Breakables should be placed out of reach if your dog is to have full run of the house. If he is to be limited to certain places within the house, keep any potentially dangerous items in the 'off-limits' areas. An electrical cord can pose a danger should the puppy decide to taste it—and who is going to convince a pup that it would not make a great chew toy? Cords should be fastened tightly against the wall. If your dog is going to spend time in a crate, make sure that there is nothing near his crate that he can reach if he sticks his curious little nose or paws through the openings. Just as you would with a child, keep all

CHEMICAL TOXINS

Scour your garage for potential puppy dangers. Remove weed killers, pesticides and antifreeze materials. Antifreeze is highly toxic and even a few drops can kill an adult dog. The sweet taste attracts the animal, who will quickly consume it from the floor or curbside.

household cleaners and chemicals where the pup cannot reach them.

It is also important to make sure that the outside of your home is safe. Of course your puppy should never be unsupervised, but a pup let loose in the garden will want to run and explore, and he should be granted that freedom. Do not let a fence give you a false sense of security; you would be surprised how crafty (and persistent) a dog

FEEDING TIP
You will probably start feeding your pup the same food that he has been getting from the breeder; the breeder should give you a few days' supply to start you off. Although you should not give your pup too many treats, you will want to have puppy treats on hand for coaxing, training, rewards, etc. Be careful, though, as a small pup's calorie requirements are relatively low and a few treats can add up to almost a full day's worth of calories without the required nutrition.

A FORTNIGHT'S GRACE
It will take at least two weeks for your puppy to become accustomed to his new surroundings. Give him lots of love, attention, handling, frequent opportunities to relieve himself, a diet he likes to eat and a place he can call his own.

can be in working out how to dig under and squeeze his way through small holes, or to jump or climb over a fence. The remedy is to make the fence well embedded into the ground and high enough so that it really is impossible for your dog to get over it (about 3 metres should suffice). Be sure to repair or secure any gaps in the fence. Check the fence periodically to ensure that it is in good shape and make repairs as needed; a very determined pup may return to the same spot to 'work on it' until he is able to get through.

FIRST TRIP TO THE VET
You have selected your puppy, and your home and family are ready. Now all you have to do is collect your Puli from the breeder and the fun begins, right? Well...not so fast. Something else you need to prepare is your pup's first trip to the veterinary surgeon. Perhaps the breeder can recommend someone in the area that

specialises in Pulik, or maybe you know some other Puli owners who can suggest a good vet. Either way, you should have an appointment arranged for your pup before you pick him up.

The pup's first visit will consist of an overall examination to make sure that the pup does not have any problems that are not apparent to the eye. The veterinary surgeon will also set up a schedule for the pup's vaccinations; the breeder will inform you of which ones the pup has already received and the vet can continue from there.

INTRODUCTION TO THE FAMILY

Everyone in the house will be excited about the puppy coming home and will want to pet him and play with him, but it is best to make the introduction low-key so as not to overwhelm the puppy. He is apprehensive already. It is the first time he has

THE TRIP HOME

Taking your dog from the breeder to your home in a car can be a very uncomfortable experience for both of you. The puppy will have been taken from his warm, friendly, safe environment and brought into a strange new environment. An environment that moves! Be prepared for loose bowels, urination, crying, whining and even fear biting. With proper love and encouragement when you arrive home, the stress of the trip should quickly disappear.

STRESS-FREE

Some experts in canine health advise that stress during a dog's early years of development can compromise and weaken his immune system and may trigger the potential for a shortened life expectancy. They emphasise the need for happy and stress-free growing-up years.

been separated from his mother and the breeder, and the ride to your home is likely to be the first time he has been in a car. The last thing you want to do is smother him, as this will only frighten him further. This is not to say that human contact is not extremely necessary at this stage, because this is the time when a connection between the pup and his human family is formed. Gentle petting and soothing words should help console him, as well as just putting him down and letting him explore on his own (under your watchful eye, of course).

The pup may approach the

PUPPY PROBLEMS

The majority of problems that are commonly seen in young pups will disappear as your dog gets older. However, how you deal with problems when he is young will determine how he reacts to discipline as an adult dog. It is important to establish who is boss (hopefully it will be you!) right away when you are first bonding with your dog. This bond will set the tone for the rest of your life together.

Pulik get along very well with all members of the family if properly socialised (introduced). Children should be taught how to handle and interact with the dog. Parents need to supervise both child and dog.

family members or may busy himself with exploring for a while. Gradually, each person should spend some time with the pup, one at a time, crouching down to get as close to the pup's level as possible and letting him sniff their hands and petting him gently. He definitely needs human attention and he needs to be touched—this is how to form an immediate bond. Just remember that the pup is experiencing a lot of things for the first time, at the same time. There are new people, new noises, new smells, and new things to investigate: so be gentle, be affectionate, and be as comforting as you can be.

PUP'S FIRST NIGHT HOME

You have travelled home with your new charge safely in his crate. He's been to the vet for a thorough check-up; he's been weighed, his papers examined; perhaps he's even been vaccinated and wormed as well. He's met the family, licked the whole family, including the excited children and the less-than-happy cat. He's explored his area, his new bed, the garden and anywhere else he's been permitted. He's eaten his first meal at home and relieved himself in the proper place. He's heard lots of new sounds, smelled new friends and seen more of the outside world than ever before.

That was just the first day! He's worn out and is ready for bed...or so you think!

It's puppy's first night and you are ready to say 'Good night'—keep in mind that this is puppy's first night ever to be sleeping alone. His dam and littermates are no longer at paw's length and he's a bit scared, cold and lonely. Be reassuring to your new family member. This is not the time to spoil him and give in to his inevitable whining.

Puppies whine. They whine to let others know where they are and hopefully to get company out of it. Place your pup in his new bed or crate in his room and close the door. Mercifully, he may fall asleep without a peep. When the

PUPPY PERSONALITY

When a litter becomes available to you, choosing a pup out of all those adorable faces will not be an easy task! Sound temperament is of utmost importance, but each pup has its own personality and some may be better suited to you than others. A feisty, independent pup will do well in a home with older children and adults, while quiet, shy puppies will thrive in a home with minimum noise and distractions. Your breeder knows the pups best and should be able to guide you in the right direction.

SOCIALISATION

Thorough socialisation includes not only meeting new people but also being introduced to new experiences such as riding in the car, having his coat brushed, hearing the television, walking in a crowd—the list is endless. The more your pup experiences, and the more positive the experiences are, the less of a shock and the less frightening it will be for your pup to encounter new things.

inevitable occurs, ignore the whining: he is fine. Be strong and keep his interest in mind. Do not allow yourself to feel guilty and visit the pup. He will fall asleep eventually.

Many breeders recommend placing a piece of bedding from his former home in his new bed so that he recognises the scent of his littermates. Others still advise placing a hot water bottle in his bed for warmth. This latter may be a good idea provided the pup doesn't attempt to suckle—he'll get good and wet and may not fall asleep so fast.

Puppy's first night can be somewhat stressful for the pup and his new family. Remember that you are setting the tone of nighttime at your house. Unless you want to play with your pup every evening at 10 p.m., midnight and 2 a.m., don't initiate the habit. Your family will thank you, and so will your pup!

Dogs of any breed that are socialised as pups will grow up to get on well with and behave politely around other dogs as adults.

PREVENTING PUPPY PROBLEMS

SOCIALISATION

Now that you have done all of the preparatory work and have helped your pup get accustomed to his new home and family, it is about time for you to have some fun! Socialising your Puli pup gives you the opportunity to show off your new friend, and your pup gets to reap the benefits of being an adorable furry creature that people will want to pet and, in general, think is absolutely precious!

Besides getting to know his new family, your puppy should be exposed to other people, animals and situations, but of course he must not come into close contact with dogs you don't know well until his course of injections is fully complete. This will help him become well adjusted as he grows up and less prone to being timid or fearful of the new things he will encounter. Your pup's socialisation began with the breeder but now it is your responsibility to continue it. The socialisation he receives up until the age of 12 weeks is the most critical, as this is the time when he forms his impressions of the outside world. Be especially careful during the eight-to-ten-week period, also known as the fear period. The interaction he receives during this time should be gentle and reassuring. Lack of socialisation can manifest itself in fear and aggression as the dog grows up. He needs lots of human contact, affection, handling and exposure to other animals.

Once your pup has received his necessary vaccinations, feel free to take him out and about (on his lead, of course). Walk him around the neighbourhood, take him on your daily errands, let people pet him, let him meet other dogs and pets, etc. Puppies do not have to try to make friends; there will be no shortage of people who will want to introduce themselves. Just make sure that you carefully supervise each meeting. If the neighbour-hood children want to say hello, for example, that is great—

> **MANNERS MATTER**
> During the socialisation process, a puppy should meet people, experience different environments and definitely be exposed to other canines. Through playing and interacting with other dogs, your puppy will learn lessons, ranging from controlling the pressure of his jaws by biting his litter mates to the inner-workings of the canine pack that he will apply to his human relationships for the rest of his life. That is why removing a puppy from its litter too early (before eight weeks) can be detrimental to the pup's development.

children and pups most often make great companions. Sometimes an excited child can unintentionally handle a pup too roughly, or an overzealous pup can playfully nip a little too hard. You want to make sociali-sation experiences positive ones. What a pup learns during this very formative stage will affect his attitude toward future encounters. You want your dog to be comfortable around everyone. A pup that has a bad experience with a child may grow up to be a dog that is shy around or aggressive toward children.

CONSISTENCY IN TRAINING

Dogs, being pack animals, naturally need a leader, or else they try to establish dominance in their packs. When you welcome a dog into your family, the choice of who becomes the leader and who becomes the 'pack' is entirely up to you! Your pup's intuitive quest for dominance, coupled with the fact that it is nearly impossible to look at an adorable Puli pup with his 'puppy-dog' eyes and not cave in, give the pup almost an unfair advantage in getting the upper hand! A pup will definitely test the waters to see what he can and cannot do. Do not give in to those pleading eyes—stand your ground when it comes to disciplining the pup

and make sure that all family members do the same. It will only confuse the pup when Mother tells him to get off the sofa when he is used to sitting up there with Father to watch the nightly news. Avoid discrep-ancies by having all members of the household decide on the rules before the pup even comes home…and be consistent in enforcing them! Early training shapes the dog's personality, so you cannot be unclear in what you expect.

COMMON PUPPY PROBLEMS

The best way to prevent puppy problems is to be proactive in stopping an undesirable behaviour as soon as it starts. The old saying 'You can't teach an old dog new tricks' does not necessarily hold true, but it is true that it is much easier to discourage bad behaviour in a young developing pup than to wait until the pup's bad behaviour becomes the adult dog's bad habit. There are some problems that are especially prevalent in puppies as they develop.

NIPPING

As puppies start to teethe, they feel the need to sink their teeth into anything available… unfortunately that includes your fingers, arms, hair and toes. You may find this behaviour cute for the first five seconds...until you feel just how sharp those puppy teeth are. This is something you want to discourage immediately and consistently with a firm 'No!' (or whatever number of firm 'No's' it takes for him to understand that you mean business). Then replace your finger with an appropriate chew toy. While this behaviour is merely annoying when the dog is young, it can become dangerous as your Puli's adult teeth grow in and his jaws develop, and he continues to think it is okay to gnaw on human appendages. Your Puli does not mean any harm with a friendly nip, but he also does not know his own strength.

CRYING/WHINING

Your pup will often cry, whine, whimper, howl or make some type of commotion when he is left alone. This is basically his way of calling out for attention to make sure that you know he is there and that you have not forgotten about him. He feels insecure when he is left alone, when you are out of the house and he is in his crate or when you are in another part of the house and he cannot see you. The noise he is making is an expression of the anxiety he feels at being alone, so he needs to be taught that being alone is okay. You are not actually

training the dog to stop making noise, you are training him to feel comfortable when he is alone and thus removing the need for him to make the noise. This is where the crate with cosy bedding and a toy comes in handy. You want to know that he is safe when you are not there to supervise, and you know that he will be safe in his crate rather than roaming freely about the house. In order for the pup to stay in his crate without making a fuss, he needs to be comfortable in his crate. On that note, it is extremely important that the crate is never used as a form of punishment, or the pup will have a negative association with the crate.

Accustom the pup to the crate in short, gradually increasing time intervals.

Everything looks tempting to a teething pup...and puppy teeth can certainly inflict pain! Discourage nipping early on and be consistent in telling your chewing puppy 'No!'

Everyday Care of Your
HUNGARIAN PULI

DIETARY AND FEEDING CONSIDERATIONS

Today the choices of food for your Puli are many and varied. There are simply dozens of brands of food in all sorts of flavours and textures, ranging from puppy diets to those for seniors. There are even hypoallergenic and low-calorie diets available. Because your Puli's food has a bearing on coat, health and temperament, it is essential that the most suitable diet is selected for a Puli of his age. It is fair to say, however, that even experienced owners can be perplexed by the enormous range of foods available. Only understanding what is best for your dog will help you reach a valued decision.

Dog foods are produced in three basic types: dried, semi-moist and tinned. Dried foods are useful for the cost-conscious for overall they tend to be less expensive than semi-moist or tinned. They also contain the least fat and the most preservatives. In general, tinned foods are made up of 60–70 percent water, while semi-moist ones often contain so much sugar that they are perhaps the least preferred by owners, even though their dogs seem to like them.

When selecting your dog's diet, three stages of development must be considered: the puppy stage, adult stage and the senior or veteran stage.

PUPPY STAGE

Puppies instinctively want to suck milk from their mother's teats and a normal puppy will exhibit this behaviour from just a few moments following birth. If puppies do not attempt to suckle within the first half-hour or so, they should be encouraged to do so by placing them on the nipples, having selected ones with plenty of milk. This early milk supply is important in providing colostrum to protect the puppies during the first eight to ten weeks of their lives.

TEST FOR PROPER DIET
A good test for proper diet is the colour, odour and firmness of your dog's stool. A healthy dog usually produces three semi-hard stools per day. The stools should have no unpleasant odour. They should be the same colour from excretion to excretion.

Although a mother's milk is much better than any milk formula, despite there being some excellent ones available, if the puppies do not feed, you will have to feed them yourself. For those with less experience, advice from a veterinary surgeon is important so that you feed not only the right quantity of milk but that of correct quality, fed at suitably frequent intervals, usually every two hours during the first few days of life.

Puppies should be allowed to nurse from their mothers for about the first six weeks, although from the third or fourth week you should begin to introduce small portions of suitable solid food. Most breeders like to introduce alternate milk and meat meals initially, building up to weaning time.

By the time the puppies are seven or a maximum of eight weeks old, they should be fully weaned and fed solely on a proprietary puppy food. Selection of the most suitable, good-quality diet at this time is essential, for a puppy's fastest growth rate is during the first year of life. Veterinary surgeons are usually able to offer advice in this regard and, although the frequency of meals will have been reduced over time, only when a young dog has reached the age of about 12 months

FOOD PREFERENCE

Selecting the best dried dog food is difficult. There is no majority consensus among veterinary scientists as to the value of nutrient analyses (protein, fat, fibre, moisture, ash, cholesterol, minerals, etc.). All agree that feeding trials are what matters, but you also have to consider the individual dog. Its weight, age, activity and what pleases its taste, all must be considered. It is probably best to take the advice of your veterinary surgeon. Every dog's dietary requirements vary, even during the lifetime of a particular dog.

If your dog is fed a good dried food, it does not require supplements of meat or vegetables. Dogs do appreciate a little variety in their diets so you may choose to stay with the same brand, but vary the flavour. Alternatively you may wish to add a little flavoured stock to give a difference to the taste.

FEEDING TIP
You must store your dried dog food carefully. Open packages of dog food quickly lose their vitamin value, usually within 90 days of being opened. Mould spores and vermin could also contaminate the food.

should an adult diet be fed.

Puppy and junior diets should be well balanced for the needs of your dog, so that except in certain circumstances additional vitamins, minerals and proteins will not be required.

Adult Diets

A dog is considered an adult when it has stopped growing, so in general the diet of a Puli can be changed to an adult one at about 10 to 12 months of age. Again you should rely upon your veterinary surgeon or

dietary specialist to recommend an acceptable maintenance diet. Major dog food manufacturers specialise in this type of food, and it is merely necessary for you to select the one best suited to your dog's needs. Active dogs may have different requirements than sedate dogs.

Senior Diets

As dogs get older, their metabolism changes. The older dog usually exercises less, moves more slowly and sleeps more. This change in lifestyle and physiological performance requires a change in diet. Since these changes take place slowly, they might not be recognisable. What is easily recognisable is weight gain. By continuing to feed your dog an adult-maintenance diet when it is slowing down metabolically, your dog

A LITTLE GOES A LONG WAY
When the course of inoculations is complete, then you will be able to take the puppy into public places. Until then, you will have to be content with little games in the garden and the start of those first collar-and-lead training sessions. Food is converted into energy and growth. If you allow excessive exercise, then growth will surely suffer. A guide in those early days is that nothing should be done in excess. Food, play, a little walk and lots of sleep are the priorities.

will gain weight. Obesity in an older dog compounds the health problems that already accompany old age.

As your dog gets older, few of his organs function up to par. The kidneys slow down and the intestines become less efficient. These age-related factors are best handled with a change in diet and a change in feeding schedule to give smaller portions that are more easily digested.

There is no single best diet for every older dog. While many dogs do well on light or senior diets, other dogs do better on puppy diets or other special premium diets such as lamb and rice. Be sensitive to your senior Puli's diet and this will help control other problems that may arise with your old friend.

WATER

Just as your dog needs proper nutrition from his food, water is an essential 'nutrient' as well. Water keeps the dog's body properly hydrated and promotes normal function of the body's systems. During housebreaking it is necessary to keep an eye on how much water your Puli is drinking, but once he is reliably trained he should have access to clean fresh water at all times, especially if you feed dried food. Make certain that the dog's water bowl is clean, and change the water often.

GRAIN-BASED DIETS

Some less expensive dog foods are based on grains and other plant proteins. While these products may appear to be attractively priced, many breeders prefer a diet based on animal proteins and believe that they are more conducive to your dog's health. Many grain-based diets rely on soy protein that may cause flatulence (passing gas).

There are many cases, however, when your dog might require a special diet. These special requirements should only be recommended by your veterinary surgeon.

EXERCISE

All dogs require some form of exercise, regardless of breed. A sedentary lifestyle is as harmful to a dog as it is to a person. The Puli is a fairly active breed that enjoys exercise, but you don't have to be an Olympic athlete! Regular walks, play sessions in the garden and letting the dog

WHAT ARE YOU FEEDING YOUR DOG?

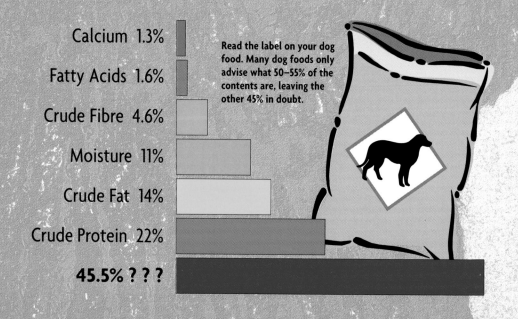

Calcium 1.3%

Fatty Acids 1.6%

Crude Fibre 4.6%

Read the label on your dog food. Many dog foods only advise what 50–55% of the contents are, leaving the other 45% in doubt.

Moisture 11%

Crude Fat 14%

Crude Protein 22%

45.5% ? ? ?

run free in the garden under your supervision are sufficient forms of exercise for the Puli. For those who are more ambitious, you will find that your Puli also enjoys long walks, an occasional hike, games of fetch or even a swim! Bear in mind that an overweight dog should never be suddenly over-exercised; instead he should be encouraged to increase exercise slowly. Not only is exercise essential to keep the dog's body fit, it is essential to his mental well-being. A bored dog will find something to do, which often manifests itself in some type of destructive behaviour. In this sense, exercise is essential for the owner's mental well-being as well!

GROOMING

One major consideration when rearing this breed is the coat. The Puli is born with a fairly closely laid jacket that soon

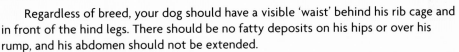

Fatty Risks

Any dog of any breed can suffer from obesity. Studies show that nearly 30 percent of our dogs are overweight, primarily from high caloric intake and low energy expenditure. The hound and gundog breeds are the most likely affected, and females are at a greater risk of obesity than males. Pet dogs that are neutered are twice as prone to obesity as intact, whole dogs.

Regardless of breed, your dog should have a visible 'waist' behind his rib cage and in front of the hind legs. There should be no fatty deposits on his hips or over his rump, and his abdomen should not be extended.

Veterinary specialists link obesity with respiratory problems, cardiac disease and liver dysfunction as well as low sperm count and abnormal oestrous cycles in breeding animals. Other complications include musculoskeletal disease (including arthritis), decreased immune competence, diabetes mellitus, hypothyroidism, pancreatitis and dermatosis. Other studies have indicated that excess fat leads to heat stress, as obese dogs cannot regulate their body temperatures as well as normal-weight dogs.

Don't be discouraged if you discover that your dog has a heart problem or a complicated neurological condition requiring special attention. It is possible to tend to his special medical needs. Veterinary specialists focus on areas such as cardiology, neurology and oncology. Veterinary medical associations require rigorous training and experience before granting certification in a speciality. Consulting a specialist may offer you greater peace of mind when seeking treatment for your dog.

EXERCISE ALERT!

You should be careful where you exercise your dog. Many countryside areas have been sprayed with chemicals that are highly toxic to both dogs and humans. Never allow your dog to eat grass or drink from puddles on either public or private grounds, as the run-off water may contain chemicals from sprays and herbicides.

begins with brushing the hair in the direction from the tail toward the head. The hair grows longer and then it will start to make attempts to go into little rat tails. It is at this stage that Mother Nature decides the formation of the future coat, and you should not try to alter it in any way. Some hairs will start to split into quite fine strands while others may be distinctly thicker. As soon as the coat indicates it is about to start cording, all brushing and combing stops. To encourage the

starts to grow and stand away from the body. Early grooming

Vitamins Recommended for Dogs

Some breeders and vets recommend the supplementation of vitamins to a dog's diet—others do not. Before embarking on a vitamin programme, consult your vet.

Vitamin / Dosage	Food source	Benefits
A / 10,000 IU/week	Eggs, butter, yoghurt, meat	Skin, eyes, hind legs, haircoat
B / Varies	Organs, cottage cheese, sardines	Appetite, fleas, heart, skin and coat
C / 2000 mg+	Fruit, legumes, leafy green vegetables	Healing, arthritis, kidneys
D / Varies	Cod liver, cheese, organs, eggs	Bones, teeth, endocrine system
E / 250 IU daily	Leafy green vegetables, meat, wheat germ oil	Skin, muscles, nerves, healing, digestion
F / Varies	Fish oils, raw meat	Heart, skin, coat, fleas
K / Varies	Naturally in body, not through food	Blood clotting

formation and firming up of the baby cords, a light spray each day with soft water can be helpful. As the embryo cords lengthen, they will normally start to thicken a little and it is at this stage that you must devote time to working your way through the whole coat, ensuring that the forming cords are separated right down to the skin. It is most important that any light fluff between the cords is plucked out, so that air can reach the skin. If the hairs at skin level are allowed to remain, they will thicken and these mats will not only prevent air getting in but also cause irritation to the skin. Indeed, in extreme cases, it can become host to some little undesirable passengers, i.e. parasites. The loose fluffy hair, if removed without delay, allows the forming cords to remain separated. The actual separation into cords can start at any time from around six months of age, and it may be almost a year before the cords are firm and separate.

Do check certain areas where there is a greater risk of felting up. Under the ear flaps, under the lower jaw, around the throat, behind the elbows and inside the hindlegs are the likely places. Check also on top of the body, where the coat comes under the tail. Varying types of cords can be within a single

DRINK, DRANK, DRUNK— MAKE IT A DOUBLE

In both humans and dogs, as well as most living organisms, water forms the major part of nearly every body tissue. Naturally, we take water for granted, but without it, life as we know it would cease.

For dogs, water is needed to keep their bodies functioning biochemically. Additionally, water is needed to replace the water lost while panting. Unlike humans who are able to sweat to dissipate heat, dogs must pant to cool down, thereby losing the vital water from their bodies needed to regulate their body temperatures. Humans lose electrolyte-containing products and other body-fluid components through sweating; dogs do not lose anything except water.

Water is essential always, but especially so when the weather is hot or humid or when your dog is exercising or working vigorously.

You will need to do at least some of your Puli's coat maintenance at home, and will need proper grooming equipment to do so.

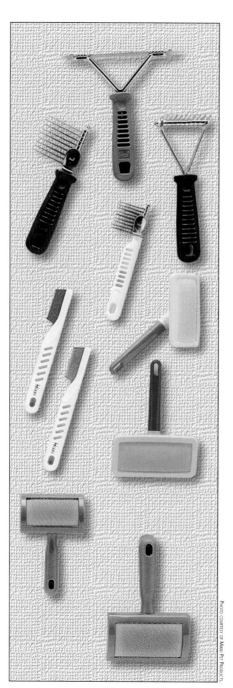

PHOTO COURTESY OF MIKKI PET PRODUCTS.

GROOMING EQUIPMENT

How much grooming equipment you purchase will depend on how much grooming you are going to do. Here are some basics:

- Natural bristle brush
- Slicker brush
- Metal comb
- Scissors
- Blaster
- Rubber mat
- Dog shampoo
- Spray hose attachment
- Ear cleaner
- Cotton wipes
- Towels
- Nail clippers

litter, and it is advised that you should not try to alter their size or shape. If you attempt to thin down a thicker cord, you will contribute to a weakening, and in time these weaker cords can become worn and fall off. A well-tended corded coat will always attract attention and admiration, and the hours spent on it in the early days will be a worthwhile investment. The consistency of cords can be likened to an old woolly garment that has started to felt up. The more you wash and rub it, the firmer it mats—that is what happens with a corded coat. Once firm and properly corded, these strands don't come undone.

A common misunder-standing of the inexperienced owner is the belief that when you put the Puli in water, all cords become undone, and then you have to knit or plait it up after every bath. Of course this is nonsense–thank heavens! There are many types of shampoos and conditioners available and we use an insecticidal shampoo, followed by a good-quality lanolin conditioner to prevent the cords' drying out and becoming discoloured. Dead hair tends to turn brown or chestnut red, and the ends of the cords, being composed of the oldest hair, will often turn brown, especially on black or grey dogs.

New owners frequently ask many questions about the Puli's coat, including whether or not Pulik moult. The answer is, not quite as other dogs do, but moulting is responsible for the formation of the Puli's cords. The cords are formed by the longer harsher hair twisting and trapping the discarded undercoat. Another question is whether Pulik get too hot under all their cords and can they feel the cold. They can get rather warm, but the coat provides natural insulation, serving to keep the strong sunshine off the body to avoid burning and to retain the body warmth, preventing wind and rain from reaching the underparts.

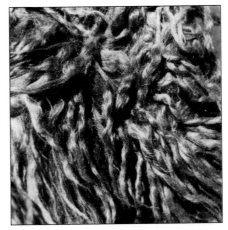

Three stages of cord development in the Puli's coat. The bottom picture shows an adult coat.

Yes, the Puli does have eyes underneath all of those cords!

Trimming the hair around the anal pore is necessary for health and hygiene reasons.

SOAP IT UP

The use of human soap products like shampoo, bubble bath and hand soap can be damaging to a dog's coat and skin. Human products are too strong and remove the protective oils coating the dog's hair and skin (making him water-resistant). Use only shampoo made especially for dogs and you may like to use a medicated shampoo, which will always help to keep external parasites at bay.

BATHING BEAUTY

Once you are sure that the dog is thoroughly rinsed, squeeze the excess water out of the coat with your hand and dry him with a heavy towel. You may choose to use a blaster on his coat or just let it dry naturally. In cold weather, never allow your dog outside with a wet coat.

There are 'dry bath' products on the market, which are sprays and powders intended for spot cleaning, that can be used between regular baths, if necessary. They are not substitutes for regular baths, but they are easy to use for touch-ups as they do not require rinsing.

The formation of the cords is a natural progression, yet still needs attention. The forming cords should be kept separate, ensuring that air can reach the skin and that any loose fluffy hairs are removed.

When our dogs are bathed, we check that anal glands are clear. The anal glands are situated on each side of the anal pore and produce a liquid that helps lubricate the dog's motions. If there is no firmness to the excreta, then the glands don't lubricate, and so they may start to build up a foul-smelling fluid accumulation. If left, the glands can become impacted, which in extreme cases can turn into an abscess, causing soreness and pain. Your vet will show you how to check and express these glands, so that with regular inspection at bath time, you should never have problems. While on the subject, we always check the hair surrounding the anus, keeping it well trimmed, so as not to become matted or clogged.

EAR CLEANING

The ears should be kept clean with a cotton wipe and ear powder made especially for dogs. Be on the lookout for any signs of infection or ear mite infestation. If your Puli has been shaking his head or scratching at his ears frequently, this usually

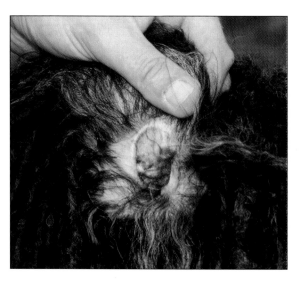

'quick' in each nail. The quick is a blood vessel that runs through the centre of each nail and grows rather close to the end. It will bleed if accidentally cut, which will be quite painful for the dog as it contains nerve endings. Keep some type of clotting agent on hand, such as a styptic pencil or styptic powder (the type used for shaving). This will stop the bleeding quickly when applied to the end of the cut nail. Do not panic if you cut the quick, just

Part of the grooming process includes cleaning your Puli's ears and checking for ear mites, odour and/or other signs of a problem.

indicates a problem. If his ears have an unusual odour, this is a sure sign of mite infestation or infection, and a signal to have his ears checked by the veterinary surgeon.

Nail Clipping

Your Puli should be accustomed to having his nails trimmed at an early age, since it will be part of your maintenance routine throughout his life. Not only does it look nicer, but long nails can scratch someone unintentionally. Also, a long nail has a better chance of ripping and bleeding, or causing the feet to spread. A good rule of thumb is that if you can hear your dog's nails clicking on the floor when he walks, his nails are too long.

Before you start cutting, make sure you can identify the

DEADLY DECAY

Did you know that periodontal disease (a condition of the bone and gums surrounding a tooth) can be fatal? Having your dog's teeth and mouth checked yearly can prevent it.

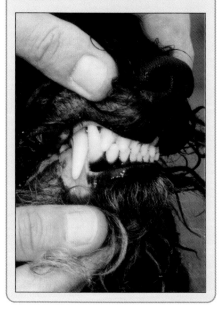

stop the bleeding and talk soothingly to your dog. Once he has calmed down, move on to the next nail. It is better to clip a little at a time, particularly with black-nailed dogs.

Hold your pup steady as you begin trimming his nails; you do not want him to make any sudden movements or run away. Talk to him soothingly and stroke him as you clip. Holding his foot in your hand, simply take off the end of each nail in one quick clip. You can purchase nail clippers that are specially made for dogs; you can probably find them wherever you buy pet or grooming supplies.

TRAVELLING WITH YOUR DOG

CAR TRAVEL

You should accustom your Puli to riding in a car at an early age. You may or may not take him in the car often, but at the very least he will need to go to the vet and you do not want these trips to be traumatic for the dog or troublesome for you. The safest way for a dog to ride in the car is in his crate. If he uses a crate in the house, you can use the same crate for travel.

Put the pup in the crate and see how he reacts. If he seems uneasy, you can have a passenger hold him on his lap

PEDICURE TIP
A dog that spends a lot of time outside on a hard surface, such as cement or pavement, will have his nails naturally worn down and may not need to have them trimmed as often, except maybe in the colder months when he is not outside as much. Regardless, it is best to get your dog accustomed to this procedure at an early age so that he is used to it. Some dogs are especially sensitive about having their feet touched, but if a dog has experienced it since he was young, he should not be bothered by it.

while you drive. Another option is a specially made safety harness for dogs, which straps the dog in much like a seat belt. Do not let the dog roam loose in the vehicle—this is very dangerous! If you should stop short, your dog can be thrown

You can purchase special nail clippers made for use on dogs. The guillotine-type, shown here, are easy to use as they remove the nail tip in one quick motion.

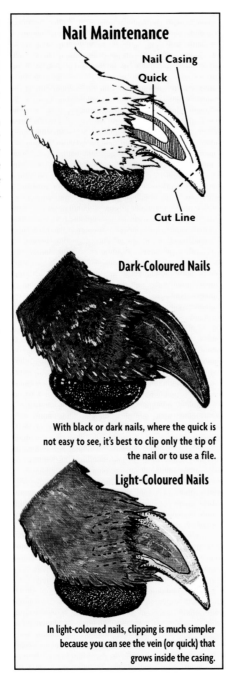

Nail Maintenance

Nail Casing

Quick

Cut Line

Dark-Coloured Nails

With black or dark nails, where the quick is not easy to see, it's best to clip only the tip of the nail or to use a file.

Light-Coloured Nails

In light-coloured nails, clipping is much simpler because you can see the vein (or quick) that grows inside the casing.

and injured. If the dog starts climbing on you and pestering you while you are driving, you will not be able to concentrate on the road. It is an unsafe situation for everyone—human and canine.

For long trips, be prepared to stop to let the dog relieve himself. Take with you whatever you need to clean up after him, including some paper kitchen towels and perhaps some old towelling for use should he have an accident in the car or suffer from travel sickness.

AIR TRAVEL

While it is possible to take a dog on a flight within Britain, this is fairly unusual and advance permission is always required. The dog will be required to travel in a fibreglass crate and you should always check in advance with the airline regarding specific requirements. To help the dog be at ease, put one of his favourite toys in the crate with him. Do not feed the dog for at least six hours before the trip to minimise his need to relieve himself. However, certain regulations specify that water must always be made available to the dog in the crate.

Make sure your dog is properly identified and that your contact information appears on his ID tags and on his crate. Animals travel in a different area of the plane than human passengers so every rule must be strictly adhered to so as to prevent the risk of getting separated from your dog.

BOARDING
So you want to take a family holiday—and you want to include all members of the family. You would probably make arrangements for accommodation ahead of time anyway, but this is especially important when travelling with a dog. You do not want to make an overnight stop at the only place around for miles and find out that they do not allow dogs. Also, you do not want to reserve a place for your family without confirming that you are travelling with a dog because if it is

against their policy you may not have a place to stay.

Alternatively, if you are travelling and choose not to bring your Puli, you will have to make arrangements for him while you are away. Some

MOTION SICKNESS
*If life is a motorway...*your dog may not want to come along for the ride! Some dogs experience motion sickness in cars that leads to excessive salivation and even vomiting. In most cases, your dog will fare better in the familiar, safe confines of his crate. To desensitise your dog, try going on several short jaunts before trying a long trip. If your dog experiences distress when riding in the vehicle, drive with him only when absolutely necessary, and do not feed him or give him water before you go.

IDENTIFICATION

If your dog gets lost, he is not able to ask for directions home.

Identification tags fastened to the collar give important information—the dog's name, the owner's name, the owner's address and a telephone number where the owner can be reached. This makes it easy for whomever finds the dog to contact the owner and arrange to have the dog returned. An added advantage is that a person will be more likely to approach a lost dog who has ID tags on his collar; it tells the person that this is somebody's pet rather than a stray. This is the easiest and fastest method of identification provided that the tags stay on the collar and the collar stays on the dog.

neighbour pop in often or stay at your house, or bring your dog to a reputable boarding kennel. If you choose to board him at a kennel, you should visit in advance to see the facilities provided, how clean they are and where the dogs are kept. Talk to some of the employees and see how they treat the dogs—do they spend time with the dogs, play with them, exercise them, etc.? Also find out the kennel's policy on vaccinations and what they require. This is for all of the dogs' safety, since when dogs are kept together, there is a greater risk of diseases being passed from dog to dog.

IDENTIFICATION

Your Puli is your valued companion and friend. That is why you always keep a close eye on him and you have made sure that he cannot escape from the garden or wriggle out of his collar and run away from you. However, accidents can happen and there may come a time when your dog unexpectedly gets separated from you. If this unfortunate event should occur, the first thing on your mind will be finding him. Proper identification, including an ID tag, a tattoo, and possibly a microchip, will increase the chances of his being returned to you safely and quickly.

options are to take him to a neighbour's house to stay while you are gone, to have a trusted

Housebreaking and Training Your
HUNGARIAN PULI

Living with an untrained dog is a lot like owning a piano that you do not know how to play—it is a nice object to look at but it does not do much more than that to bring you pleasure. Now try taking piano lessons and suddenly the piano comes alive and brings forth magical sounds and rhythms that set your heart singing and your body swaying.

The same is true with your Puli. Any dog is a big responsibility and if not trained sensibly may develop unacceptable behaviour that annoys you or could even cause family friction.

To train your Puli, you may like to enrol in an obedience class. Teach him good manners as you learn how and why he behaves the way he does. Find out how to communicate with your dog and how to recognise and understand his communications with you. Suddenly the dog takes on a new role in your life—he is clever, interesting, well-behaved and fun to be with. He demonstrates his bond of devotion to you daily. In other words, your Puli does wonders for your ego because he constantly reminds you that you are not only his leader, you are his hero!

Those involved with teaching

REAP THE REWARDS
If you start with a normal, healthy dog and give him time, patience and some carefully executed lessons, you will reap the rewards of that training for the life of the dog. And what a life it will be! The two of you will find immeasurable pleasure in the companionship you have built together with love, respect and understanding.

dog obedience and counselling owners about their dogs' behaviour have discovered some interesting facts about dog ownership. For example, training dogs when they are puppies results in the highest rate of success in developing well-mannered and well-adjusted adult dogs. Training an older dog, from six months to six years of age, can produce almost equal results providing that the owner accepts the dog's slower rate of learning capability and is willing to work patiently to help the dog succeed at developing to his fullest potential. Unfortunately, many owners of untrained adult dogs lack the patience factor, so they do not persist until their dogs are

You mould your pup's behaviour from the first day you bring him home. His natural curiosity can get him into trouble; you must set the rules, both for his safety and your sanity.

> ### THE HAND THAT FEEDS
> To a dog's way of thinking, your hands are like his mouth in terms of a defence mechanism. If you squeeze him too tightly, he might just bite you because that would be his normal response. This is not aggressive biting and, although all biting should be discouraged, you need the discipline in learning how to handle your dog.

successful at learning particular behaviours.

Training a puppy aged 10 to 16 weeks (20 weeks at the most) is like working with a dry sponge in a pool of water. The pup soaks up whatever you show him and constantly looks for more things to do and learn. At this early age, his body is not yet producing hormones, and therein lies the reason for such a high rate of success. Without hormones, he is focused on his owners and not particularly interested in investigating other places, dogs, people, etc. You are his leader: his provider of food, water, shelter and security. He latches onto you and wants to stay close. He will usually follow you from room to room, will not let you out of his sight when you are outdoors with him and will respond in like manner to the people and animals you encounter. If you greet a friend warmly, he will be happy to greet the person as well. If,

however, you are hesitant, even anxious, about the approach of a stranger, he will respond accordingly.

Once the puppy begins to produce hormones, his natural curiosity emerges and he begins to investigate the world around him. It is at this time when you may notice that the untrained dog begins to wander away from you and even ignore your commands to stay close. When this behaviour becomes a problem, the owner has two choices: get rid of the dog or train him. It is strongly urged that you choose the latter option.

There are usually classes within a reasonable distance from the owner's home, but you can also do a lot to train your dog yourself. Sometimes there are classes available but the tuition is too costly. Whatever the circumstances, the solution to the problem of lack of lesson availability lies within the pages of this book.

This chapter is devoted to helping you train your Puli at home. If the recommended procedures are followed faithfully, you may expect positive results that will prove rewarding both to you and your dog.

Whether your new charge is a puppy or a mature adult, the methods of teaching and the techniques we use in training basic behaviours are the same. After all, no dog, whether puppy

PARENTAL GUIDANCE

Training a dog is a life experience. Many parents admit that much of what they know about raising children they learned from caring for their dogs. Dogs respond to love, fairness and guidance, just as children do. Become a good dog owner and you may become an even better parent.

or adult, likes harsh or inhumane methods. All creatures, however, respond favourably to gentle motivational methods and sincere praise and encouragement. Now let us get started.

THINK BEFORE YOU BARK

Dogs are sensitive to their master's moods and emotions. Use your voice wisely when communicating with your dog. Never raise your voice at your dog unless you are angry and trying to correct him. 'Barking' at your dog can become as meaning-less as 'dogspeak' is to you. Think before you bark!

HOUSEBREAKING

You can train a puppy to relieve itself wherever you choose, but this must be somewhere suitable. You should bear in mind from the outset that when your puppy is old enough to go out in public places, any canine deposits must be removed at once. You will always have to carry with you a small plastic bag or 'poop-scoop.'

Outdoor training includes such surfaces as grass, soil and cement. Indoor training usually means training your dog to newspaper.

When deciding on the surface and location that you will want your Puli to use, be sure it is going to be permanent. Training your dog to grass and then changing your mind two months later is extremely difficult for both dog and owner.

Next, choose the command you will use each and every time you want your puppy to void. 'Hurry up' and 'Toilet' are examples of commands commonly used by dog owners.

Get in the habit of giving the puppy your chosen relief command before you take him out. That way, when he becomes an adult, you will be able to determine if he wants to go out when you ask him. A confirmation will be signs of interest, wagging his tail, watching you intently, going to the door, etc.

PUPPY'S NEEDS

Puppy needs to relieve himself after play periods, after each meal, after he has been sleeping and at any time he indicates that he is looking for a place to urinate or defecate.

The urinary and intestinal tract muscles of very young puppies are not fully developed. Therefore, like human babies, puppies need to relieve themselves frequently.

Take your puppy out often— every hour for an eight-week-old, for example, and always immediately after sleeping and eating. The older the puppy, the less often he will need to relieve himself. Finally, as a mature healthy adult, he will require only three to five relief trips per day.

HOUSING

Since the types of housing and control you provide for your puppy have a direct relationship on the success of housetraining, we consider the various aspects of both before we begin training.

Taking a new puppy home and turning him loose in your house can be compared to turning a child loose in a sports arena and telling the child that the place is all his! The sheer enormity of the place would be too much for him to handle.

Instead, offer the puppy clearly defined areas where he can play, sleep, eat and live. A room

HONOUR AND OBEY

Dogs are the most honourable animals in existence. They consider another species (humans) as their own. They interface with you. You are their leader. Puppies perceive children to be on their level; their actions around small children are different from their behaviour around their adult masters.

of the house where the family gathers is the most obvious choice. Puppies are social animals and need to feel a part of the pack right from the start. Hearing your voice, watching you while you are doing things and smelling you nearby are all positive reinforcers that he is now a member of your pack. Usually a family room, the

Crate training is becoming a widely used method of housebreaking and training dogs. A wire crate, as shown here, is popular for use inside the home, as it affords the dog a view of what is going on around him.

TRAINING TIP

Dogs will do anything for your attention. If you reward the dog when he is calm and resting, you will develop a well-mannered dog. If, on the other hand, you greet your dog excitedly and encourage him to wrestle with you, the dog will greet you the same way and you will have a hyperactive dog on your hands.

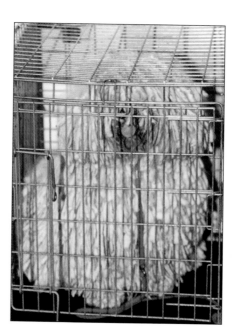

kitchen or a nearby adjoining breakfast area is ideal for providing safety and security for both puppy and owner.

Within that room there should be a smaller area that the puppy can call his own. An alcove, a wire or fibreglass dog crate or a

It's amazing how a treat or a favourite chew toy can hold a pup's attention during a training lesson!

MEALTIME

Mealtime should be a peaceful time for your puppy. Do not put his food and water bowls in a high-traffic area in the house. For example, give him his own little corner of the kitchen where he can eat undisturbed and where he will not be underfoot. Do not allow small children or other family members to disturb the pup when he is eating.

CANINE DEVELOPMENT SCHEDULE

It is important to understand how and at what age a puppy develops into adulthood. If you are a puppy owner, consult the following Canine Development Schedule to determine the stage of development your puppy is currently experiencing. This knowledge will help you as you work with the puppy in the weeks and months ahead.

Period	Age	Characteristics
FIRST TO THIRD	**BIRTH TO SEVEN WEEKS**	Puppy needs food, sleep and warmth, and responds to simple and gentle touching. Needs mother for security and disciplining. Needs littermates for learning and interacting with other dogs. Pup learns to function within a pack and learns pack order of dominance. Begin socialising with adults and children for short periods. Begins to become aware of its environment.
FOURTH	**EIGHT TO TWELVE WEEKS**	Brain is fully developed. Needs socialising with outside world. Remove from mother and littermates. Needs to change from canine pack to human pack. Human dominance necessary. Fear period occurs between 8 and 16 weeks. Avoid fright and pain.
FIFTH	**THIRTEEN TO SIXTEEN WEEKS**	Training and formal obedience should begin. Less association with other dogs, more with people, places, situations. Period will pass easily if you remember this is pup's change-to-adolescence time. Be firm and fair. Flight instinct prominent. Permissiveness and over-disciplining can do permanent damage. Praise for good behaviour.
JUVENILE	**FOUR TO EIGHT MONTHS**	Another fear period about 7 to 8 months of age. It passes quickly, but be cautious of fright and pain. Sexual maturity reached. Dominant traits established. Dog should understand sit, down, come and stay by now.

NOTE: THESE ARE APPROXIMATE TIME FRAMES. ALLOW FOR INDIVIDUAL DIFFERENCES IN PUPPIES.

TAKE THE LEAD

Do not carry your dog to his toilet area. Lead him there on a leash or, better yet, encourage him to follow you to the spot. If you start carrying him to his spot, you might end up doing this routine forever and your dog will have the satisfaction of having trained YOU.

fenced (not boarded!) corner from which he can view the activities of his new family will be fine. The size of the area or crate is the key factor here. The area must be large enough for the puppy to lie down and stretch out as well as stand up without rubbing his head on the top, yet small enough so that he cannot relieve himself at one end and sleep at the other without coming into contact with his droppings until fully trained to relieve himself outside.

Dogs are, by nature, clean animals and will not remain close to their relief areas unless forced to do so. In those cases, they then become dirty dogs and usually remain that way for life.

The designated area should contain clean bedding and a toy. Water must always be available, in a non-spill container.

Control

By control, we mean helping the puppy to create a lifestyle pattern that will be compatible to that of his human pack (YOU!). Just as we guide little children to learn our way of life, we must show the puppy when it is time to play, eat, sleep, exercise and even entertain himself.

Your puppy should always sleep in his crate. He should also learn that, during times of household confusion and excessive human activity such as at breakfast when family members

THE GOLDEN RULE

The golden rule of dog training is simple. For each 'question' (command), there is only one correct answer (reaction). One command = one reaction. Keep practising the command until the dog reacts correctly without hesitating. Be repetitive but not monotonous. Dogs get bored just as people do!

are preparing for the day, he can play by himself in relative safety and comfort in his designated area. Each time you leave the puppy alone, he should understand exactly where he is to stay. Puppies are chewers. They cannot tell the difference between lamp cords, television wires, shoes, table legs, etc. Chewing into a television wire, for example, can be fatal to the puppy while a shorted wire can start a fire in the house.

If the puppy chews on the arm of the chair when he is alone, you will probably discipline him angrily when you get home. Thus, he makes the association that your coming home means he is going to be punished. (He will not remember chewing the chair and is incapable of making the association of the discipline with his naughty deed.)

Other times of excitement, such as family parties, etc., can be

PRACTICE MAKES PERFECT!

- Have training lessons with your dog every day in several short segments—three to five times a day for a few minutes at a time is ideal.
- Do not have long practice sessions. The dog will become easily bored.
- Never practise when you are tired, ill, worried or in an otherwise negative mood. This will transmit to the dog and may have an adverse effect on its performance.

Think fun, short and above all POSITIVE! End each session on a high note, rather than a failed exercise, and make sure to give a lot of praise. Enjoy the training and help your dog enjoy it, too.

THE SUCCESS METHOD

Success that comes by luck is usually short lived. Success that comes by well-thought-out proven methods is often more easily achieved and permanent. This is the Success Method. It is designed to give you, the puppy owner, a simple yet proven way to help your puppy develop clean living habits and a feeling of security in his new environment.

fun for the puppy providing he can view the activities from the security of his designated area. He is not underfoot and he is not being fed all sorts of titbits that will probably cause him stomach distress, yet he still feels a part of the fun.

SCHEDULE

A puppy should be taken to his relief area each time he is released from his designated area, after meals, after a play session and when he first awakens in the

THE SUCCESS METHOD

1 Tell the puppy 'Crate time!' and place him in the crate with a small treat (a piece of cheese or half of a biscuit). Let him stay in the crate for five minutes while you are in the same room. Then release him and praise lavishly. Never release him when he is fussing. Wait until he is quiet before you let him out.

2 Repeat Step 1 several times a day.

3 The next day, place the puppy in the crate as before. Let him stay there for ten minutes. Do this several times.

4 Continue building time in five-minute increments until the puppy

stays in his crate for 30 minutes with you in the room. Always take him to his relief area after prolonged periods in his crate.

5 Now go back to Step 1 and let the puppy stay in his crate for five minutes, this time while you are out of the room.

6 Once again, build crate time in five-minute increments with you out of the room. When the puppy will stay willingly in his crate (he may even fall asleep!) for 30 minutes with you out of the room, he will be ready to stay in it for several hours at a time.

6 Steps to Successful Crate Training

morning (at age eight weeks, this can mean 5 a.m.!). The puppy will indicate that he's ready 'to go' by circling or sniffing busily—do not misinterpret these signs. For a puppy less than ten weeks of age, a routine of taking him out every hour is necessary. As the puppy grows, he will be able to wait for longer periods of time.

Keep trips to his relief area short. Stay no more than five or six minutes and then return to the house. If he goes during that time, praise him lavishly and take him indoors immediately. If he does not, but he has an accident when you go back indoors, pick him up immediately, say 'No! No!' and return to his relief area. Wait a few minutes, then return to the house again. Never hit a puppy or rub his face in urine or excrement when he has had an accident!

Once indoors, put the puppy in his crate until you have had time to clean up his accident. Then release him to the family area and watch him more closely than before. Chances are, his accident was a result of your not picking up his signal or waiting too long before offering him the opportunity to relieve himself. Never hold a grudge against the puppy for accidents.

Let the puppy learn that going outdoors means it is time to relieve himself, not play. Once trained, he will be able to play indoors and out and still differen-

HOW MANY TIMES A DAY?

AGE	RELIEF TRIPS
To 14 weeks	10
14–22 weeks	8
22–32 weeks	6
Adulthood (dog stops growing)	4

These are estimates, of course, but they are a guide to the MINIMUM opportunities a dog should have each day to relieve itself.

tiate between the times for play versus the times for relief.

Help him develop regular hours for naps, being alone,

playing by himself and just resting, all in his crate. Encourage him to entertain himself while you are busy with your activities. Let him learn that having you near is comforting, but it is not your main purpose in life to provide him with undivided attention.

Each time you put a puppy in his own area, use the same command, whatever suits best.

HOUSEBREAKING TIP

Most of all, be consistent. Always take your dog to the same location, always use the same command, and always have him on lead when he is in his relief area, unless a fenced-in garden is available.

By following the Success Method, your puppy will be completely housetrained by the time his muscle and brain development reach maturity. Keep in mind that small breeds usually mature faster than large breeds, but all puppies should be trained by six months of age.

THE CLEAN LIFE

By providing sleeping and resting quarters that fit the dog, and offering frequent opportunities to relieve himself outside his quarters, the puppy quickly learns that the outdoors (or the newspaper if you are training him to paper) is the place to go when he needs to urinate or defecate. It also reinforces his innate desire to keep his sleeping quarters clean. This, in turn, helps develop the muscle control that will eventually produce a dog with clean living habits.

Soon he will run to his crate or special area when he hears you say those words.

Crate training provides safety for you, the puppy and the home. It also provides the puppy with a feeling of security, and that helps the puppy achieve self-confidence and clean habits.

Remember that one of the primary ingredients in housetraining your puppy is control. Regardless of your lifestyle, there will always be occasions when you will need to have a place where your dog can stay and be happy and safe. Crate training is the answer for now and in the future.

In conclusion, a few key elements are really all you need for a successful housetraining method—consistency, frequency, praise, control and supervision. By following these procedures with a normal, healthy puppy, you and the puppy will soon be past the stage of 'accidents' and ready to move on to a full and rewarding life together.

ROLES OF DISCIPLINE, REWARD AND PUNISHMENT

Discipline, training one to act in accordance with rules, brings order to life. It is as simple as that. Without discipline, particularly in a group society, chaos reigns supreme and the group will eventually perish. Humans and canines are social animals and need some form of discipline in order to function effectively. They must procure food, protect their home base and their young and reproduce to keep the species going.

If there were no discipline in the lives of social animals, they would eventually die from starvation and/or predation by other stronger animals.

In the case of domestic canines, dogs need discipline in their lives in order to understand how their pack (you and other family members) functions and how they must act in order to survive.

A large humane society in a highly populated area recently surveyed dog owners regarding their satisfaction with their

ATTENTION!
Your dog is actually training you at the same time you are training him. Dogs do things to get attention. They usually repeat whatever succeeds in getting your attention.

PLAN TO PLAY

The puppy should also have regular play and exercise sessions when he is with you or a family member. Exercise for a very young puppy can consist of a short walk around the house or garden. Playing can include fetching games with a large ball or a special raggy. (All puppies teethe and need soft things upon which to chew.) Remember to restrict play periods to indoors within his living area (the family room, for example) until he is completely housetrained.

relationships with their dogs. People who had trained their dogs were 75% more satisfied with their pets than those who had never trained their dogs.

Dr Edward Thorndike, a psychologist, established *Thorndike's Theory of Learning*, which states that a behaviour that results in a pleasant event tends to be repeated. A behaviour that results in an unpleasant event tends not to be repeated. It is this theory on which training methods are based today. For example, if you manipulate a dog to perform a specific behaviour and reward him for doing it, he is likely to do it again because he enjoyed the end result.

Occasionally, punishment, a penalty inflicted for an offence, is necessary. The best type of punishment often comes from an outside source. For example, a child is told not to touch the stove because he may get burned. He disobeys and touches the stove. In doing so, he receives a burn. From that time on, he respects the heat of the stove and avoids contact with it. Therefore, a behaviour that results in an unpleasant event tends not to be repeated.

A good example of a dog learning the hard way is the dog who chases the house cat. He is told many times to leave the cat

TRAINING RULES

If you want to be successful in training your dog, you have four rules to obey yourself:
1. Develop an understanding of how a dog thinks.
2. Do not blame the dog for lack of communication.
3. Define your dog's personality and act accordingly.
4. Have patience and be consistent.

alone, yet he persists in teasing the cat. Then, one day he begins chasing the cat but the cat turns and swipes a claw across the dog's face, leaving him with a painful gash on his nose. The final result is that the dog stops chasing the cat.

TRAINING EQUIPMENT

COLLAR AND LEAD

Pulik are quite determined and self-willed little creatures and will probably object to both collar and lead! A first step is to put on a lightweight collar for just a few minutes. After a few futile attempts to scratch it off, they will soon forget it and you can gradually increase the time that it is left on. The next step is to attach a light lead that the pup will probably not notice, until you

OPEN MINDS
Dogs are as different from each other as people are. What works for one dog may not work for another. Have an open mind. If one method of training is unsuccessful, try another.

'NO' MEANS 'NO!'
Dogs do not understand our language. They can be trained to react to a certain sound, at a certain volume. If you say 'No, Oliver' in a very soft pleasant voice it will not have the same meaning as 'No, Oliver!!' when you shout it as loud as you can. You should never use the dog's name during a reprimand, just the command NO!! Since dogs don't understand words, comics often use dogs trained with opposite meanings. Thus, when the comic commands his dog to SIT the dog will stand up, and vice versa.

attempt to lead them along. The reaction will probably be like a little bucking bronco, but gentle coaxing words will surely help, coupled with gentle pulling to make them accept that you are in charge. After a while they will stop pulling against you and should start to come along in the same direction. Soon they will accept that this collar and lead training can be fun, and will start to trot alongside you. When the immunity from the injections has built up, they will be ready for short walks outside the home area. It can be a great temptation to make early walks rather lengthy, as any proud owner will want to show off their new Puli. Please do remember that you have

The selection of the proper collar and lead is important for the safety and comfort of your Puli.

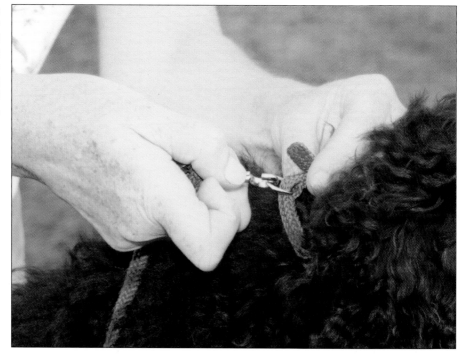

a very young animal that still has lots of growing to do, and that to overtire them will inhibit growth. When you embark on the first walk, choose somewhere that is comparatively quiet with few diversions. They will naturally be curious about the surroundings and need to gain confidence being in a strange place. To suddenly expose them to lots of people, traffic and other dogs can be rather overwhelming so these outings should be taken calmly and in quiet places. Let them become confident and gradually encounter diversions. While you are walking, they will eventually come to see other dogs being walked. Don't allow them to dash across to them as some will try. You will have no idea of the reaction of the other dog, which could be protective or aggressive.

TREATS

Have a bag of treats on hand. Something nutritious and easy to swallow works best. Use a soft treat, a chunk of cheese or a piece of cooked chicken rather than a dry biscuit. By the time the dog has finished chewing a dry treat, he will forget why he is being rewarded in the first place! Using food rewards will not teach a dog to beg at the table—the only way to teach a dog to beg at the table is to give him food from the table. In training, rewarding the dog with a food treat will help him associate praise and the treats with learning new behaviours that obviously please his owner.

TRAINING BEGINS: ASK THE DOG A QUESTION

In order to teach your dog anything, you must first get his attention. After all, he cannot learn anything if he is looking away from you with his mind on something else.

To get his attention, ask him, 'School?' and immediately walk over to him and give him a treat as you tell him 'Good dog.' Wait a minute or two and repeat the routine, this time with a treat in your hand as you approach within a foot of the dog. Do not go directly to him, but stop about a foot short of him and hold out the treat as you ask, 'School?' He will see you approaching with a treat in your hand and most likely begin walking toward you. As you meet, give him the treat and praise again.

The third time, ask the question, have a treat in your hand and walk only a short distance toward the dog so that he must walk almost all the way to you. As he reaches you, give him the treat and praise again.

By this time, the dog will probably be getting the idea that if he pays attention to you, especially when you ask that question, it will pay off in treats and enjoyable activities for him. In other words, he learns that 'school' means doing great things with you that are fun and result in positive attention for him.

Remember that the dog does not understand your verbal language; he only recognises sounds. Your question translates to a series of sounds for him, and those sounds become the signal to go to you and pay attention; if he does, he will get to interact with you plus receive treats and praise.

THE BASIC COMMANDS

TEACHING SIT

Now that you have the dog's attention, attach his lead and hold it in your left hand and a food treat in your right. Place your food hand at the dog's nose and let him lick the treat but not take it from you. Say 'Sit' and slowly raise your food hand from in front of the dog's nose up over his head so that he is looking at the ceiling. As he bends his head upward, he will have to bend his knees to maintain his balance. As he bends his knees, he will assume a sit position. At that point, release the food treat and praise lavishly with comments such as 'Good dog! Good sit!,' etc. Remember to always praise enthusiastically, because dogs relish verbal praise from their owners and feel so proud of themselves whenever they accomplish a behaviour.

You will not use food forever in getting the dog to obey your commands. Food is only used to teach new behaviours, and once the dog knows what you want when you give a specific command, you will wean him off the food treats but still maintain the verbal praise. After all, you will always have your voice with you, and there will be many times when you have no food rewards but expect the dog to obey.

TEACHING DOWN

Teaching the down exercise is easy when you understand how the dog perceives the down position, and it is very difficult when you do not. Dogs perceive the down position as a submissive one, therefore teaching the down exercise using a forceful method can sometimes make the dog develop such a fear of the down that he either runs away when you say 'Down' or he attempts to snap at the person who tries to force him down.

Have the dog sit close alongside your left leg, facing in the same direction as you are. Hold the lead in your left hand and a food treat in your right. Now place your left hand lightly on the top of the dog's shoulders where they meet above the spinal cord. Do not push down on the dog's shoulders; simply rest your left hand there so you can guide the dog to lie down close to your left leg rather than to swing away from your side when he drops.

Now place the food hand at the dog's nose, say 'Down' very softly (almost a whisper), and slowly lower the food hand to the dog's front feet. When the food hand reaches the floor, begin moving it forward along the floor in front of the dog. Keep talking softly to the dog, saying things like, 'Do you want this treat? You can do this, good dog.' Your reassuring tone of voice will help calm the dog as

DOUBLE JEOPARDY

A dog in jeopardy never lies down. He stays alert on his feet because instinct tells him that he may have to run away or fight for his survival. Therefore, if a dog feels threatened or anxious, he will not lie down. Consequently, it is important to have the dog calm and relaxed as he learns the down exercise.

he tries to follow the food hand in order to get the treat.

When the dog's elbows touch the floor, release the food and praise softly. Try to get the dog to maintain that down position for several seconds before you let him sit up again. The goal here is to get the dog to settle down and not feel threatened in the down position.

TEACHING STAY

It is easy to teach the dog to stay in either a sit or a down position. Again, we use food and praise during the teaching process as we help the dog to understand exactly what it is that we are expecting him to do.

To teach the sit/stay, start with the dog sitting on your left side as before and hold the lead in your left hand. Have a food treat in your right hand and place your food hand at the dog's nose. Say 'Stay' and step out on your right foot to stand directly in front of the dog, toe to toe, as he licks and nibbles the treat. Be sure to keep his head facing upward to maintain the sit position. Count to five and then swing around to stand next to the dog again with him on your left. As soon as you get back to the original position, release the food and praise lavishly.

To teach the down/stay, do the down as previously described. As soon as the dog lies down, say

'Stay' and step out on your right foot just as you did in the sit/stay. Count to five and then return to stand beside the dog with him on

HOW TO WEAN THE 'TREAT HOG'

If you have trained your dog by rewarding him with a treat each time he performs a command, he may soon decide that without the treat, he won't sit, stay or come. The best way to fix this problem is to start asking your dog to do certain commands twice before being rewarded. Slowly increase the number of commands given and then vary the number: three sits and a treat one day, five sits for a biscuit the next day. Your dog will soon realise that there is no set number of sits before he gets his reward, and he'll likely do it the first time you ask in the hope of being rewarded sooner rather than later.

your left side. Release the treat and praise as always.

Within a week or ten days, you can begin to add a bit of distance between you and your dog when you leave him. When you do, use your left hand open with the palm facing the dog as a stay signal, much the same as the hand signal a constable uses to stop traffic at an intersection.

'COME' ... BACK

Never call your dog to come to you for a correction or scold him when he reaches you. That is the quickest way to turn a 'Come' command into 'Go away fast!' Dogs think only in the present tense, and your dog will connect the scolding with coming to you, not with the misbehaviour of a few moments earlier.

Hold the food treat in your right hand as before, but this time the food is not touching the dog's nose. He will watch the food hand and quickly learn that he is going to get that treat as soon as you return to his side.

When you can stand 1 metre away from your dog for 30 seconds, you can then begin building time and distance in both stays. Eventually, the dog can be expected to remain in the stay position for prolonged periods of time until you return to him or call him to you. Always praise lavishly when he stays.

TEACHING COME

If you make teaching 'come' an exciting experience, you should never have a 'student' that does not love the game or that fails to come when called. The secret, it seems, is never to teach the word 'come.'

At times when an owner most wants his dog to come when called, the owner is likely to be upset or anxious and he allows these feelings to come through in the tone of his voice when he calls his dog. Hearing that desperation in his owner's voice, the dog fears the results of going to him and therefore either disobeys outright or runs in the opposite direction. The secret, therefore, is to teach the dog a game and, when you want him to come to you, simply play the game. It is practically a no-fail solution!

To begin, have several members of your family take a few food treats and each go into a different room in the house. Take turns calling the dog, and each person should celebrate the dog's finding him with a treat and lots of happy praise. When a person calls the dog, he is actually inviting the dog to find him and get a treat as a reward for 'winning.'

A few turns of the 'Where are you?' game and the dog will understand that everyone is playing the game and that each person has a big celebration awaiting his success at locating them. Once he learns to love the game, simply calling out 'Where are you?' will bring him running from wherever he is when he hears that all-important question.

The come command is recognised as one of the most important things to teach a dog, but there are trainers who work with thousands of dogs and never teach the actual word 'Come.' Yet these dogs will race to respond to a person who uses the dog's name followed by 'Where are you?' For example, a woman has a 12-year-old companion dog who went blind, but who never fails to locate her owner when asked, 'Where are you?'

Children, in particular, love to play this game with their dogs. Children can hide in smaller

THE STUDENT'S STRESS TEST

During training sessions you must be able to recognise signs of stress in your dog such as:

- tucking his tail between his legs
- lowering his head
- shivering or trembling
- standing completely still or running away
- panting and/or salivating
- avoiding eye contact
- flattening his ears back
- urinating submissively
- rolling over and lifting a leg
- grinning or baring teeth
- aggression when restrained

If your four-legged student displays these signs he may just be nervous or intimidated. The training session may have been too lengthy with not enough praise and affirmation. Stop for the day and try again tomorrow.

TRAINING TIP

If you are walking your dog and he suddenly stops and looks straight into your eyes, ignore him. Pull the leash and lead him into the direction you want to walk.

TEACHING HEEL

Heeling means that the dog walks beside the owner without pulling. It takes time and patience on the owner's part to succeed at teaching the dog that he (the owner) will not proceed unless the dog is walking calmly beside him. Pulling out ahead on the lead is definitely not acceptable.

Begin by holding the lead in your left hand as the dog sits beside your left leg. Move the loop end of the lead to your right hand but keep your left hand short on the lead so it keeps the dog in close next to you.

Say 'Heel' and step forward on your left foot. Keep the dog close to you and take three steps. Stop and have the dog sit next to you in what we now call the 'heel position.' Praise verbally, but do not touch the dog. Hesitate a moment and begin again with 'Heel,' taking three steps and stopping, at which point the dog is told to sit again.

Your goal here is to have the dog walk those three steps without pulling on the lead. Once he will walk calmly beside you for three steps without pulling, increase the number of steps you take to five. When he will walk politely beside you while you take five steps, you can increase the length of your walk to ten steps. Keep increasing the length of your stroll until the dog will walk quietly beside you without

places like a shower or bath, behind a bed or under a table. The dog needs to work a little bit harder to find these hiding places, but when he does he loves to celebrate with a treat and a tussle with a favourite youngster.

pulling as long as you want him to heel. When you stop heeling, indicate to the dog that the exercise is over by verbally praising as you pet him and say 'OK, good dog.' The 'OK' is used as a release word meaning that the exercise is finished and the dog is free to relax.

If you are dealing with a dog who insists on pulling you around, simply 'put on your brakes' and stand your ground until the dog realises that the two of you are not going anywhere until he is beside you and moving at your pace, not his. It may take some time just standing there to convince the dog that you are the leader and you will be the one to decide on the direction and speed of your travel.

Each time the dog looks up at you or slows down to give a slack lead between the two of you, quietly praise him and say, 'Good heel. Good dog.' Eventually, the dog will begin to respond and within a few days he will be walking politely beside you without pulling on the lead. At

HEELING WELL
Teach your dog to HEEL in an enclosed area. Once you think the dog will obey reliably and you want to attempt advanced obedience exercises such as off-lead heeling, test him in a fenced-in area so he cannot run away.

TUG OF WALK?
If you begin teaching the heel by taking long walks and letting the dog pull you along, he misinterprets this action as an acceptable form of taking a walk. When you pull back on the lead to counteract his pulling, he reads that tug as a signal to pull even harder!

first, the training sessions should be kept short and very positive; soon the dog will be able to walk nicely with you for increasingly longer distances. Remember also to give the dog free time and the opportunity to run and play when you have finished heel practice.

WEANING OFF FOOD IN TRAINING

Food is used in training new behaviours. Once the dog understands what behaviour goes with a specific command, it is time to start weaning him off the food treats. At first, give a treat after each exercise. Then, start to give a treat only after every other exercise. Mix up the times when you offer a food reward and the times when you only offer praise so that the dog will never know when he is going to receive both food and praise and when he is going to receive only praise. This is called a variable ratio reward system and it proves successful because there is always the chance that the owner will produce a

> ### COMMAND STANCE
> Stand up straight and authoritatively when giving your dog commands. Do not issue commands when lying on the floor or lying on your back on the sofa. If you are on your hands and knees when you give a command, your dog will think you are positioning yourself to play.

> ### OBEDIENCE SCHOOL
> A basic obedience beginner's class usually lasts for six to eight weeks. Dog and owner attend an hour-long lesson once a week and practise for a few minutes, several times a day, each day at home. If done properly, the whole procedure will result in a well-mannered dog and an owner who delights in living with a pet that is eager to please and enjoys doing things with his owner.

treat, so the dog never stops trying for that reward. No matter what, ALWAYS give verbal praise.

OBEDIENCE CLASSES

It is a good idea to enrol in an obedience class if one is available in your area. If yours is a show dog, ringcraft classes would be more appropriate. Many areas have dog clubs that offer basic obedience training as well as preparatory classes for obedience competition. There are also local dog trainers who offer similar classes.

At working trials, dogs can earn titles at various levels of competition. The beginning levels of competition include basic behaviours such as sit, down, heel, etc. The more advanced levels of competition include jumping, retrieving, scent discrimination and signal work. The advanced levels require a dog and owner to put a lot of time and effort into their training and the titles that can be earned at these levels of competition are very prestigious.

OTHER ACTIVITIES FOR LIFE

Whether a dog is trained in the structured environment of a class or alone with his owner at home, there are many activities that can bring fun and rewards to both owner and dog once they have mastered basic control.

Teaching the dog to help out around the home, in the garden or on the farm provides great satisfaction to both dog and owner. In addition, the dog's help makes life a little easier for his owner and raises his stature as a valued companion to his family. It helps give the dog a purpose by occupying his mind and providing an outlet for his energy.

If you are interested in participating in organised competition with your Puli, there are activities other than obedience in which you and your dog can become involved. Agility is a popular sport where dogs run through an obstacle course that includes various jumps, tunnels and other exercises to test the dog's speed and coordination. The owners run beside their dogs to give commands and to guide them through the course. Although competitive, the focus is on fun—it's fun to do, fun to watch and great exercise.

HELPING PAWS

Your dog may not be the next Lassie, but every pet has the potential to do some tricks well. Identify his natural talents and hone them. Is your dog always happy and upbeat? Teach him to wag his tail or give you his paw on command. Real homebodies can be trained to do household chores, such as carrying dirty washing or retrieving the morning paper.

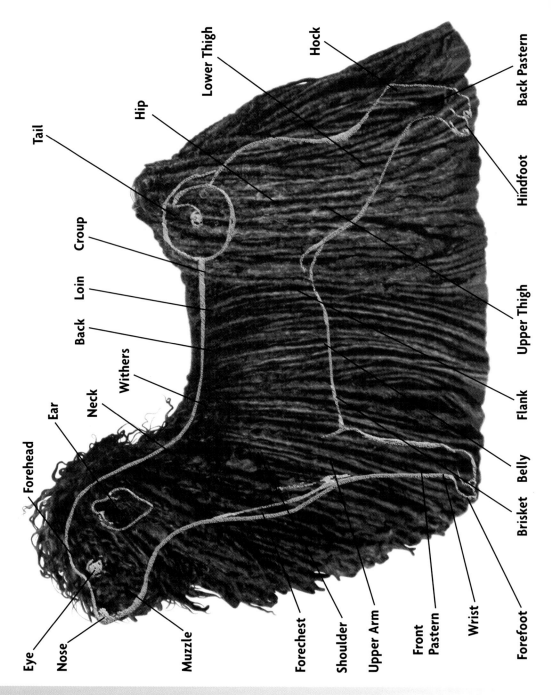

Physical Structure of the Hungarian Puli

The Puli is certainly the healthiest breed that we have owned and bred. Apart from collecting worming tablets, our dogs normally see the vet on an annual basis for their booster injections. We have always checked ears and kept loose hair plucked to ensure cleanliness, and clipped nails as needed. If you cannot cope with such basic care, then you will need to visit your vet or a local dog groomer who can undertake these simple tasks for you.

Dogs suffer many of the same physical illnesses as people. They might even share many of the same psychological problems. Since people usually know more about human diseases than canine maladies, many of the terms used in this chapter will be familiar but not necessarily those used by veterinary surgeons. We will use the term *x-ray*, instead of the more acceptable term *radiograph*. We will also use the familiar term *symptoms* even though dogs don't have symptoms, which are verbal descriptions of the patient's feelings; dogs have clinical signs. Since dogs can't speak, we have to look for *clinical signs*...but we still use the term *symptoms* in this book.

As a general rule, medicine is *practised*. That term is not arbitrary. Medicine is a constantly changing art as we learn more and more about genetics, electronic aids (like CAT scans) and daily laboratory advances. There are many dog maladies, like canine hip dysplasia, which are not universally treated in the same manner. Some veterinary surgeons opt for surgery more often than others do.

SELECTING A VETERINARY SURGEON
Your selection of a veterinary surgeon should not be based upon personality (as most are) but upon their convenience to your home. You want a vet who

Before you buy a dog, meet and interview the veterinary surgeons in your area. Take everything into consideration: discuss background, specialities, fees, emergency policies, etc.

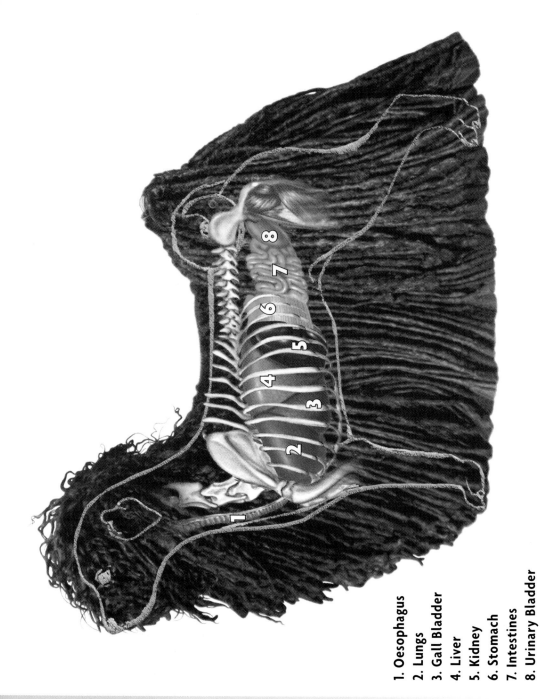

1. Oesophagus
2. Lungs
3. Gall Bladder
4. Liver
5. Kidney
6. Stomach
7. Intestines
8. Urinary Bladder

Internal Organs of the Hungarian Puli

is close because you might have emergencies or need to make multiple visits for treatments. You want a vet who has services that you might require such as tattooing and grooming, as well as sophisticated pet supplies and a good reputation for ability and responsiveness. There is nothing more frustrating than having to wait a day or more to get a response from your veterinary surgeon.

All veterinary surgeons are licensed and their diplomas and/or certificates should be displayed in their waiting rooms. There are, however, many veterinary specialities that usually require further studies and internships. There are specialists in heart problems (veterinary cardiologists), skin problems (veterinary dermatologists), teeth and gum problems (veterinary dentists), eye problems (veterinary ophthalmologists) and x-rays (veterinary radiologists), as well as vets who have specialities in bones, muscles or other organs. Most veterinary surgeons do routine surgery such as neutering, stitching up wounds and docking tails for those breeds in which such is required for show purposes. When the problem affecting your dog is serious, it is not unusual or impudent to get another medical opinion, although in Britain you are obliged to advise the vets

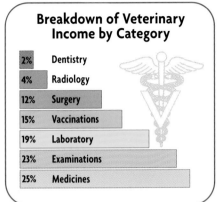

Breakdown of Veterinary Income by Category

2%	Dentistry
4%	Radiology
12%	Surgery
15%	Vaccinations
19%	Laboratory
23%	Examinations
25%	Medicines

A typical American vet's income, categorised according to services provided. This survey dealt with small-animal practices.

concerned about this. You might also want to compare costs among several veterinary surgeons. Sophisticated health care and veterinary services can be very costly. Important decisions are often based upon financial considerations.

PREVENTATIVE MEDICINE
It is much easier, less costly and more effective to practise preventative medicine than to fight bouts of illness and disease. Properly bred puppies come from parents who were selected based upon their genetic disease profile. Their mothers should have been vaccinated, free of all internal and external parasites and properly nourished. For these reasons, a visit to the veterinary surgeon who cared for the dam is recommended. The dam can pass on disease resistance to her puppies, which can last for eight to ten weeks. She can also pass on

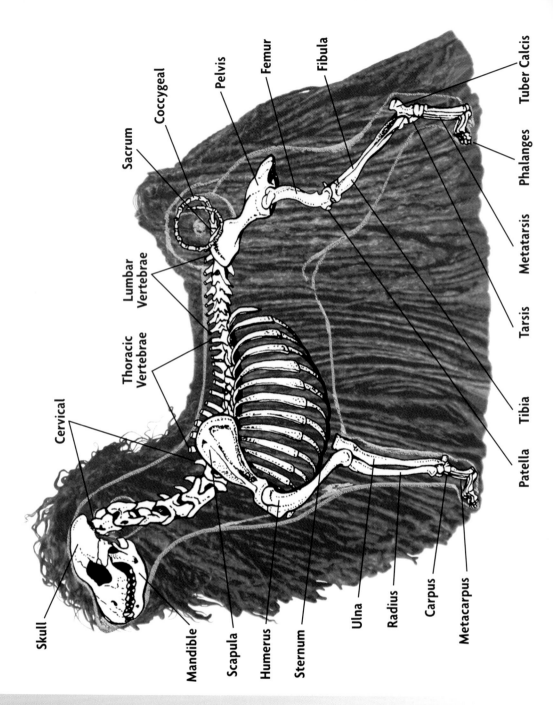

Skeletal Structure of the Hungarian Puli

parasites and many infections. That's why you should visit the veterinary surgeon who cared for the dam.

VACCINATION SCHEDULING

Most vaccinations are given by injection and should only be done by a veterinary surgeon. Both he and you should keep a record of the date of the injection, the identification of the vaccine and the amount given. Some vets give a first vaccination at eight weeks, but most dog breeders prefer the course not to commence until about ten weeks because of negating any antibodies passed on by the dam. The vaccination scheduling is usually based on a 15-day cycle. You must take your vet's advice regarding when to vaccinate as this may differ according to the vaccine used. Most vaccinations immunize your puppy against viruses.

The usual vaccines contain immunizing doses of several different viruses such as distemper, parvovirus, parainfluenza and hepatitis although some veterinary surgeons recommend separate vaccines for each disease. There are other vaccines available when the puppy is at risk. You should rely upon professional advice. This is especially true for the booster-shot programme. Most vaccination programmes require a booster when the puppy is a year old and

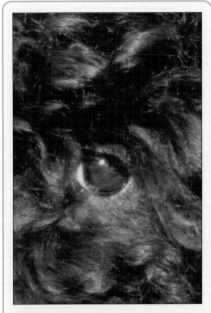

CHECK HIS EYES

Do check your Puli's eyes every single day. Nature's way of cleaning is a slight watery discharge should any dust or foreign matter cause irritation. This is likely to accumulate in the corner of the eye, where it will dry out into a hard clump. If neglected, this can lead to a gumming up with resultant soreness.

once a year thereafter. In some cases, circumstances may require more or less frequent immunizations. Kennel cough, more formally known as tracheobronchitis, is treated with a vaccine that is sprayed into the dog's nostrils. Kennel cough is usually included in routine vaccination,

HEALTH AND VACCINATION SCHEDULE

Age in Weeks:	6th	8th	10th	12th	14th	16th	20-24th	1 yr
Worm Control	✔	✔	✔	✔	✔	✔	✔	
Neutering								✔
Heartworm*		✔		✔		✔	✔	
Parvovirus	✔		✔		✔		✔	✔
Distemper		✔		✔		✔		✔
Hepatitis		✔		✔		✔		✔
Leptospirosis								✔
Parainfluenza	✔		✔		✔			✔
Dental Examination		✔					✔	✔
Complete Physical		✔					✔	✔
Coronavirus				✔			✔	✔
Kennel Cough	✔							
Hip Dysplasia								✔
Rabies*							✔	

Vaccinations are not instantly effective. It takes about two weeks for the dog's immune system to develop antibodies. Most vaccinations require annual booster shots. Your veterinary surgeon should guide you in this regard.
*Not applicable in the United Kingdom

but this is often not so effective as for other major diseases.

WEANING TO FIVE MONTHS OLD
Puppies should be weaned by the time they are about two months old. A puppy that remains for at least eight weeks with its mother and littermates usually adapts better to other dogs and people later in its life.

Some new owners have their puppy examined by a veterinary surgeon immediately, which is a good idea. Vaccination programmes usually begin when the puppy is very young.

The puppy will have its teeth examined and have its skeletal conformation and general health checked prior to certification by the veterinary surgeon. Puppies in certain breeds have problems with their kneecaps, cataracts and other

DID YOU KNOW?
Male dogs are neutered. The operation removes the testicles and requires that the dog be anaesthetised. Recovery takes about one week. Females are spayed. This is major surgery and it usually takes a bitch two weeks to recover.

VACCINE ALLERGIES
Vaccines do not work all the time. Sometimes dogs are allergic to them and many times the antibodies, which are supposed to be stimulated by the vaccine, just are not produced. You should keep your dog in the veterinary clinic for an hour after it is vaccinated to be sure there are no allergic reactions.

eye problems, heart murmurs and undescended testicles. They may also have personality problems

and your veterinary surgeon might have training in temperament evaluation.

FIVE TO TWELVE MONTHS OF AGE
Unless you intend to breed or show your dog, neutering the puppy at six months of age is recommended. Discuss this with your veterinary surgeon. Neutering has proven to be extremely beneficial to both male and female puppies. Besides eliminating the possibility of pregnancy, it inhibits (but does

DISEASE REFERENCE CHART

	What is it?	What causes it?	Symptoms
Leptospirosis	Severe disease that affects the internal organs; can be spread to people.	A bacterium, which is often carried by rodents, that enters through mucous membranes and spreads quickly throughout the body.	Range from fever, vomiting and loss of appetite in less severe cases to shock, irreversible kidney damage and possibly death in most severe cases.
Rabies	Potentially deadly virus that infects warm-blooded mammals. Not seen in United Kingdom.	Bite from a carrier of the virus, mainly wild animals.	1st stage: dog exhibits change in behaviour, fear. 2nd stage: dog's behaviour becomes more aggressive. 3rd stage: loss of coordination, trouble with bodily functions.
Parvovirus	Highly contagious virus, potentially deadly.	Ingestion of the virus, which is usually spread through the faeces of infected dogs.	Most common: severe diarrhoea. Also vomiting, fatigue, lack of appetite.
Kennel cough	Contagious respiratory infection.	Combination of types of bacteria and virus. Most common: *Bordetella bronchiseptica* bacteria and parainfluenza virus.	Chronic cough.
Distemper	Disease primarily affecting respiratory and nervous system.	Virus that is related to the human measles virus.	Mild symptoms such as fever, lack of appetite and mucous secretion progress to evidence of brain damage, 'hard pad.'
Hepatitis	Virus primarily affecting the liver.	Canine adenovirus type I (CAV-1). Enters system when dog breathes in particles.	Lesser symptoms include listlessness, diarrhoea, vomiting. More severe symptoms include 'blue-eye' (clumps of virus in eye).
Coronavirus	Virus resulting in digestive problems.	Virus is spread through infected dog's faeces.	Stomach upset evidenced by lack of appetite, vomiting, diarrhoea.

Normal hairs of a dog enlarged 200 times original size. The cuticle (outer covering) is clean and healthy. Unlike human hair that grows from the base, a dog's hair also grows from the end, as shown in the inset. Scanning electron micrographs by Dr Dennis Kunkel, University of Hawaii.

MORE THAN VACCINES

Vaccinations help prevent your new puppy from contracting diseases, but they do not cure them. Proper nutrition as well as parasite control keep your dog healthy and less susceptible to many dangerous diseases. Remember that your dog depends on you to ensure his well-being.

not prevent) breast cancer in bitches and prostate cancer in male dogs. Under no circumstances should a bitch be spayed prior to her first season.

Your veterinary surgeon should provide your puppy with a thorough dental evaluation at six months of age, ascertaining whether all the permanent teeth have erupted properly. A home dental care regimen should be initiated at six months, including brushing weekly and providing good dental devices (such as nylon bones). Regular dental care promotes healthy teeth, fresh breath and a longer life.

ONE TO SEVEN YEARS OF AGE

Once a year, your grown dog should visit the vet for an examination and vaccination boosters, if needed. Some vets recommend blood tests, thyroid level check and dental evaluation to accompany these annual visits. A thorough clinical evaluation by

COMMON PULI PROBLEMS

Pulik experience a number of common problems that can be managed by their owners. Bad breath, though uncommon, requires that the owner check the dog's mouth. Decayed teeth should be removed as they can cause bad breath and poison the digestive system. Take care of your Puli's teeth by providing proper chewing devices, including hard bones, and by having your veterinary surgeon clean his teeth annually or semi-annually.

Diarrhoea can be caused by overfeeding, wrong type of food, or food too rich in content. Starvation is the first step and then only small drinks of cooled boiled water to which you may add a little glucose and a pinch of salt to assist rehydration. If the problem does not clear up within 24 hours, consult your vet.

Grass seeds can be an annual problem with heavily coated breeds. They can penetrate the skin if not detected, tending to collect on the head and around the eyes due to the Puli's natural curiosity in sniffing around when being walked. Another vulnerable spots for grass seeds is between the toes. If left undetected, they could lead to the formation of an abscess.

the vet can provide critical background information for your dog. Blood tests are often performed at one year of age, and dental examinations around the third or fourth birthday. In the long run, quality preventative care for your pet can save money, teeth and lives.

SKIN PROBLEMS IN PULIK

Veterinary surgeons are consulted by dog owners for skin problems more than any other group of diseases or maladies. Dogs' skin is almost as sensitive as human skin and both suffer almost the same ailments. (Though the occurrence of acne in dogs is rare!) For this reason, veterinary dermatology has developed into a speciality practised by many veterinary surgeons.

Since many skin problems have visual symptoms that are almost identical, it requires the skill of an experienced veterinary dermatologist to identify and cure many of the more

severe skin disorders. Pet shops sell many treatments for skin problems but most of the treatments are directed at symptoms and not the underlying problem(s). If your dog is suffering from a skin disorder, you should seek professional assistance as quickly as possible. As with all diseases, the earlier a problem is identified and treated, the more successful is the cure.

HEREDITARY SKIN DISORDERS

Veterinary dermatologists are currently researching a number of skin disorders that are believed to have a hereditary basis. These inherited diseases

---

KNOW WHEN TO POSTPONE A VACCINATION

While the visit to the vet is costly, it is never advisable to update a vaccination when visiting with a sick or pregnant dog. Vaccinations should be avoided for all elderly dogs. If your dog is showing the signs of any illness or any medical condition, no matter how serious or mild, including skin irritations, do not vaccinate. Likewise, a lame dog should never be vaccinated; any dog undergoing surgery, or a dog on any immunosuppressant drugs should not be vaccinated until fully recovered.

PUPPY VACCINATIONS

Your veterinary surgeon will probably recommend that your puppy be vaccinated before you take him outside. There are airborne diseases, parasite eggs in the grass and unexpected visits from other dogs that might be dangerous to your puppy's health.

are transmitted by both parents, who appear (phenotypically) normal but have a recessive gene for the disease, meaning that they carry, but are not affected by, the disease. These diseases pose serious problems to breeders because in some instances there is no method of identifying carriers. Often the secondary diseases associated with these skin conditions are even more debilitating than the disorder itself, including cancers and respiratory problems; others can be lethal.

Among the hereditary skin disorders, for which the mode of inheritance is known, are: acrodermatitis, cutaneous asthenia (Ehlers-Danlos syndrome), sebaceous adenitis, cyclic hematopoiesis, dermato-myositis, IgA deficiency, colour dilution alopecia and nodular dermatofibrosis. Some of these disorders are limited to one or two breeds and others affect a large number of breeds. All inherited diseases must be diagnosed and treated by a veterinary specialist.

A SKUNKY PROBLEM

Have you noticed your dog dragging his rump along the floor? If so, it is likely that his anal sacs are impacted or possibly infected. The anal sacs are small pouches located on both sides of the anus under the skin and muscles. They are about the size and shape of a grape and contain a foul-smelling liquid. Their contents are usually emptied when the dog has a bowel movement, but if they are not emptied completely, they will impact, which will cause your dog a lot of pain. Fortunately, your veterinary surgeon can tend to this problem easily by draining the sacs for the dog. Be aware that your dog might also empty his anal sacs in cases of extreme fright.

THE SAME ALLERGIES

Chances are that you and your dog will have the same allergies. Your allergies are readily recognisable and usually easily treated. Your dog's allergies may be masked.

PARASITE BITES

Many of us are allergic to insect bites. The bites itch, erupt and may even become infected. Dogs have the same reaction to fleas, ticks and/or mites. When an insect lands on you, you have the chance to whisk it away with your hand. Unfortunately, when your dog is bitten by a flea, tick or mite, it can only scratch it away or bite it. By the time the dog has been bitten, the parasite has done some of its damage. It may also have laid eggs to cause further problems in the near future. The itching from parasite bites is probably due to the saliva injected into the site when the parasite sucks the dog's blood.

AUTO-IMMUNE SKIN CONDITIONS

Auto-immune skin conditions are commonly referred to as being allergic to yourself, while allergies are usually inflammatory reactions to an outside stimulus. Auto-immune diseases cause serious damage to the tissues that are involved.

The best known auto-immune disease is lupus, which affects people as well as dogs. The symptoms are variable and may affect the kidneys, bones, blood chemistry and skin. It can be fatal to both dogs and humans, though it is not thought to be transmissible. It is usually successfully treated with cortisone, prednisone or a similar corticosteroid, but extensive use of these drugs can have harmful side effects.

ACRAL LICK GRANULOMA

Many large dogs have a very poorly understood syndrome called acral lick granuloma. The manifestation of the problem is the dog's tireless attack at a specific area of the body, almost always the legs or paws. They lick so intensively that they remove the hair and skin, leaving an ugly, large wound. Tiny protuberances, which are outgrowths of new capillaries, bead on the surface of the wound. Owners who notice their dogs' biting and chewing at their extremities should have the vet determine the cause. If lick granuloma is identified, although there is no absolute cure, corticosteroids are the most common treatment.

AIRBORNE ALLERGIES

Another interesting allergy is pollen allergy. Humans have hay fever, rose fever and other fevers with which they suffer during the pollinating season. Many dogs suffer the same allergies. When the pollen count is high, your dog might suffer but don't expect him to sneeze and have a runny nose like humans. Dogs react to pollen allergies the same way they react to fleas—they scratch and bite themselves.

Dogs, like humans, can be tested for allergens. Discuss the testing with your veterinary dermatologist.

FOOD PROBLEMS

FOOD ALLERGIES

Dogs are allergic to many foods that are best-sellers and highly recommended by breeders and veterinary surgeons. Changing the brand of food that you buy may not eliminate the problem if the element to which the dog is allergic is contained in the new brand.

Recognising a food allergy is difficult. Humans vomit or have rashes when they eat a food to which they are allergic. Dogs neither vomit nor (usually) develop a rash. They react in the same manner as they do to an airborne or flea allergy; they itch, scratch and bite, thus making the diagnosis extremely difficult. While pollen allergies and parasite bites are usually seasonal, food allergies are year-round problems.

FOOD INTOLERANCE

Food intolerance is the inability of the dog to completely digest certain foods. Puppies that may have done very well on their mother's milk may not do well on cow's milk. The rest of this food intolerance may be loose bowels, passing gas and stomach pains. These are the only obvious symptoms of food intolerance and that makes diagnosis difficult.

TREATING FOOD PROBLEMS

It is possible to handle food allergies and food intolerance yourself. Put your dog on a diet that it has never had. Obviously if it has never eaten this new food it can't have been allergic or intolerant of it. Start with a single ingredient that is not in the dog's diet at the present time. Ingredients like chopped beef or fish are common in dogs' diets, so try something more exotic like rabbit, pheasant or even just vegetables. Keep the dog on this diet (with no additives) for a month. If the symptoms of food allergy or intolerance disappear, chances are your dog has a food allergy.

Don't think that the single ingredient cured the problem. You still must find a suitable diet and ascertain which ingredient in the old diet was objectionable. This is most easily done by adding ingredients to the new diet one at a time. Let the dog stay on the modified diet for a month before you add another ingredient. Eventually, you will determine the ingredient that caused the adverse reaction.

An alternative method is to carefully study the ingredients in the diet to which your dog is allergic or intolerant. Identify the main ingredient in this diet and eliminate the main ingredient by buying a different food that does not have that ingredient. Keep experimenting until the symptoms disappear after one month on the new diet.

EXTERNAL PARASITES

Of all the problems to which dogs are prone, none is more well known and frustrating than fleas. Flea infestation is relatively simple to cure but difficult to prevent. Parasites that are harboured inside the body are a bit more difficult to eradicate but they are easier to control.

FLEAS

To control a flea infestation you have to understand the flea's life cycle. Fleas are often thought of as a summertime problem but centrally heated homes have changed the patterns and fleas can be found at any time of the year. The most effective method of flea control is a two-stage approach: one stage to kill the adult fleas, and the other to control the development of pre-adult fleas. Unfortunately, no single active ingredient is effective against all stages of the life cycle.

LIFE CYCLE STAGES

During its life, a flea will pass through four life stages: egg, larva, pupa and adult. The adult stage is the most visible and irritating stage of the flea life cycle and this is why the majority of flea-control products concentrate on this stage.

A scanning electron micrograph (S. E. M.) of a dog flea, *Ctenocephalides canis*.

S. E. M. BY DR DENNIS KUNKEL, UNIVERSITY OF HAWAII

Magnified head of a dog flea, *Ctenocephalides canis*.

S. E. M. BY DR DENNIS KUNKEL, UNIVERSITY OF HAWAII

A Look at Fleas

Fleas have been around for millions of years and have adapted to changing host animals. They are able to go through a complete life cycle in less than one month or they can extend their lives to almost two years by remaining as pupae or cocoons. They do not need blood or any other food for up to 20 months.

They have been measured as being able to jump 300,000 times and can jump 150 times their length in any direction including straight up. Those are just a few of the reasons why they are so successful in infesting a dog!

The fact is that adult fleas account for only 1% of the total flea population, and the other 99% exist in pre-adult stages, i.e. eggs, larvae and pupae. The pre-adult stages are barely visible to the naked eye.

THE LIFE CYCLE OF THE FLEA
Eggs are laid on the dog, usually in quantities of about 20 or 30, several times a day. The female adult flea must have a blood meal before each egg-laying session. When first laid, the eggs will cling to the dog's fur, as the eggs are still moist. However, they will quickly dry out and fall from the dog, especially if the dog moves around or scratches. Many eggs will fall off in the dog's favourite area or an area in which he spends a lot of time, such as his bed.

Once the eggs fall from the dog onto the carpet or furniture, they will hatch into larvae. This takes from one to ten days. Larvae are not particularly mobile, and will usually travel only a few inches from where they hatch. However, they do have a tendency to move away from light and heavy traffic—under furniture and behind doors are common places to find high quantities of flea larvae.

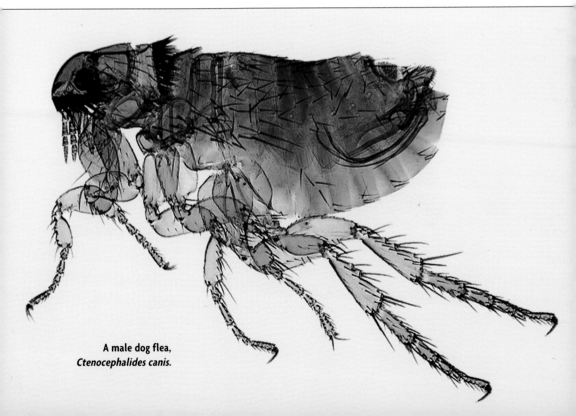

A male dog flea,
Ctenocephalides canis.

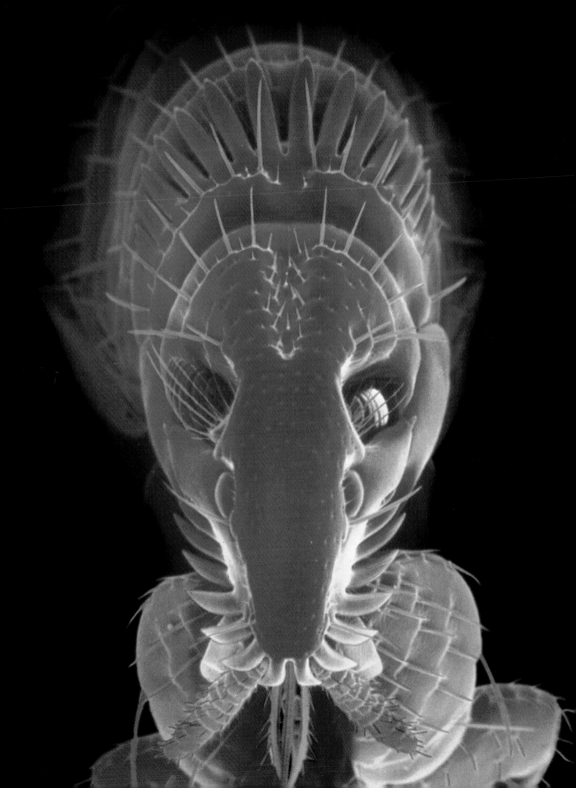

The flea larvae feed on dead organic matter, including adult flea faeces, until they are ready to change into adult fleas. Fleas will usually remain as larvae for around seven days. After this period, the larvae will pupate into protective pupae. While inside the pupae, the larvae will undergo metamorphosis and change into adult fleas. This can take as little time as a few days, but the adult fleas can remain inside the pupae waiting to hatch for up to two years. The pupae are signalled to hatch by certain stimuli, such as physical pressure—the pupae's being stepped on, heat from an animal lying on the pupae or increased carbon dioxide levels and vibrations—indicating that a suitable host is available.

Once hatched, the adult flea must feed within a few days. Once the adult flea finds a host, it will not leave voluntarily. It only becomes dislodged by grooming or the host animal's scratching. The adult flea will remain on the host for the duration of its life unless forcibly removed.

> **DID YOU KNOW?**
> Never mix flea control products without first consulting your veterinary surgeon. Some products can become toxic when combined with others and can cause serious or fatal consequences.

> **DID YOU KNOW?**
> Flea-killers are poisonous. You should not spray these toxic chemicals on areas of a dog's body that he licks, on his genitals or on his face. Flea killers taken internally are a better answer, but check with your vet in case internal therapy is not advised for your dog.

TREATING THE ENVIRONMENT AND THE DOG

Treating fleas should be a two-pronged attack. First, the environment needs to be treated; this includes carpets and furniture, especially the dog's bedding and areas underneath furniture. The environment should be treated with a household spray containing an Insect Growth Regulator (IGR) and an insecticide to kill the adult fleas. Most IGRs are effective against eggs and larvae; they actually mimic the fleas' own hormones and stop the eggs and larvae from developing into adult fleas. There are currently no treatments available to attack the pupa stage of the life cycle, so the adult insecticide is used to kill the newly hatched adult fleas before they find a host. Most IGRs are active for many months, whilst adult insecticides are only active for a few days.

When treating with a household spray, it is a good idea to vacuum before applying the

Opposite page:
A scanning electron micrograph of a dog or cat flea, *Ctenocephalides*, magnified more than 100x. This image has been colorized for effect.

The Life Cycle of the Flea

Eggs

Larva

Pupa

Adult

Photos courtesy of Fleabusters; Rx for Fleas.

Flea Control

IGR (INSECT GROWTH REGULATOR)

Two types of products should be used when treating fleas—a product to treat the pet and a product to treat the home. Adult fleas represent less than 1% of the flea population. The pre-adult fleas (eggs, larvae and pupae) represent more than 99% of the flea population and are found in the environment; it is in the case of pre-adult fleas that products containing an Insect Growth Regulator (IGR) should be used in the home.

IGRs are a new class of compounds used to prevent the development of insects. They do not kill the insect outright, but instead use the insect's biology against it to stop it from completing its growth. Products that contain methoprene are the world's first and leading IGRs. Used to control fleas and other insects, this type of IGR will stop flea larvae from developing and protect the house for up to seven months.

EN GARDE:
CATCHING FLEAS OFF GUARD!

Consider the following ways to arm yourself against fleas:
• Add a small amount of pennyroyal or eucalyptus oil to your dog's bath. These natural remedies repel fleas.
• Supplement your dog's food with fresh garlic (minced or grated) and a hearty amount of brewer's yeast, both of which ward off fleas.
• Use a flea comb on your dog daily. Submerge fleas in a cup of bleach to kill them quickly.
• Confine the dog to only a few rooms to limit the spread of fleas in the home.
• Vacuum daily...and get all of the crevices! Dispose of the bag every few days until the problem is under control.
• Wash your dog's bedding daily. Cover cushions where your dog sleeps with towels, and wash the towels often.

product. This stimulates as many pupae as possible to hatch into adult fleas. The vacuum cleaner should also be treated with a flea treatment to prevent the eggs and larvae that have been hoovered into the vacuum bag from hatching.

The second stage of treatment is to apply an adult insecticide to the dog. Traditionally, this would be in the form of a collar or a spray, but more recent innovations include digestible insecticides that poison the fleas when they ingest the dog's blood. Alternatively, there are drops that, when placed on the back of the animal's neck, spread throughout the fur and skin to kill adult fleas.

PHOTO BY DWIGHT R KUHN

Dwight R Kuhn's magnificent action photo showing a flea jumping from a dog's back.

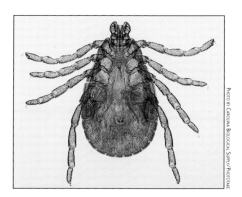

PHOTO BY CAROLINA BIOLOGICAL SUPPLY/PHOTOTAKE

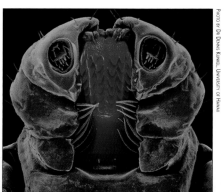

PHOTO BY DR DENNIS KUNKEL, UNIVERSITY OF HAWAII

TICKS AND MITES

Though not as common as fleas, ticks and mites are found all over the tropical and temperate world. They don't bite, like fleas; they harpoon. They dig their sharp proboscis (nose) into the dog's skin and drink the blood. Their only food and drink is dog's blood. Dogs can get Lyme disease, Rocky Mountain spotted fever (normally found in the US only), paralysis and many other diseases from ticks and mites. They may live where fleas are found and they like to hide in cracks or seams in walls wherever dogs live. They are controlled the same way fleas are controlled.

A brown dog tick, *Rhipicephalus sanguineus*, is an uncommon but annoying tick found on dogs.

The head of a dog tick, *Dermacentor variabilis*, enlarged and coloured for effect.

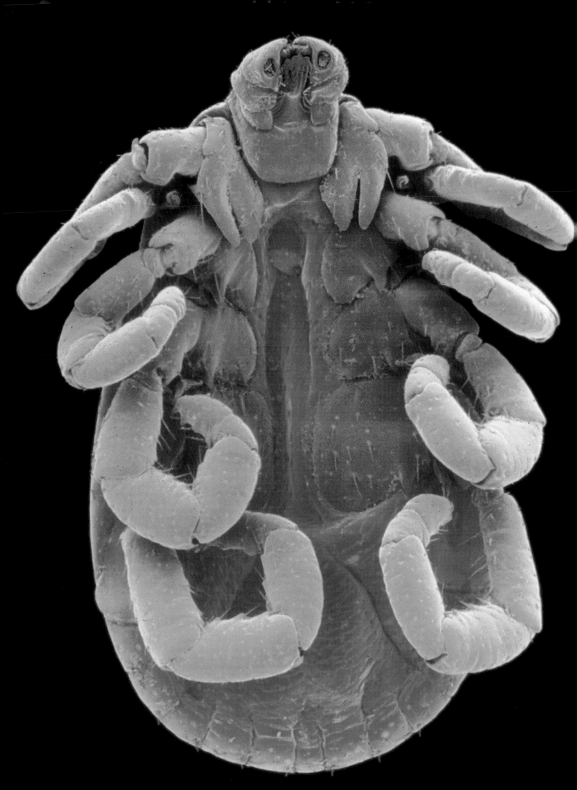

The dog tick, *Dermacentor variabilis*, may well be the most common dog tick in many geographical areas, especially those areas where the climate is hot and humid.

Most dog ticks have life expectancies of a week to six months, depending upon climatic conditions. They can neither jump nor fly, but they can crawl slowly and can range up to 5 metres (16 feet) to reach a sleeping or unsuspecting dog.

BEWARE THE DEER TICK

The great outdoors may be fun for your dog, but it also is a home to dangerous ticks. Deer ticks carry a bacterium known as *Borrelia burgdorferi* and are most active in the autumn and spring. When infections are caught early, penicillin and tetracycline are effective antibiotics, but if left untreated the bacteria may cause neurological, kidney and cardiac problems as well as long-term trouble with walking and painful joints.

Opposite page: The dog tick, *Dermacentor variabilis*, is probably the most common tick found on dogs. Look at the strength in its eight legs! No wonder it's hard to detach them.

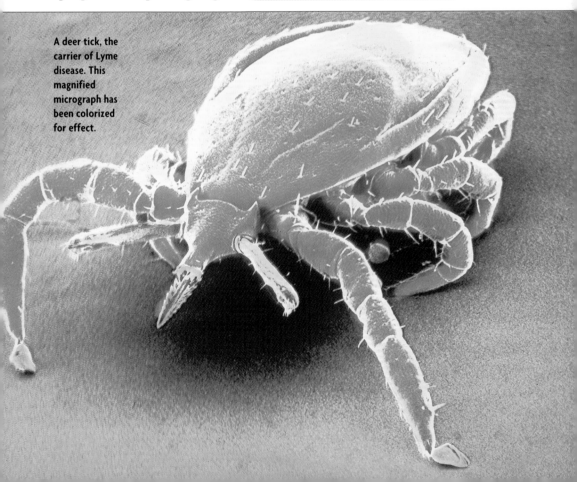

A deer tick, the carrier of Lyme disease. This magnified micrograph has been colorized for effect.

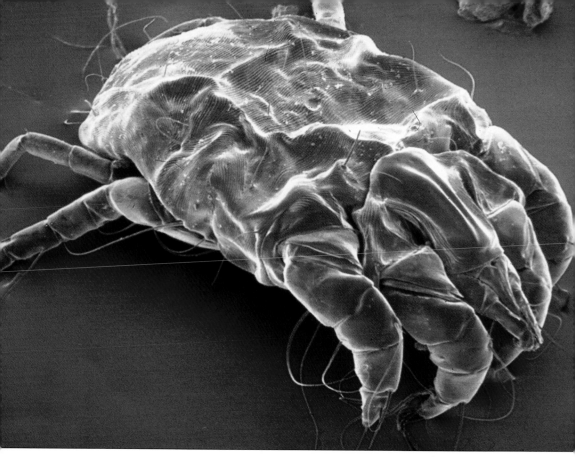

The mange mite, *Psoroptes bovis*.

Human lice look like dog lice; the two are closely related.

MANGE

Mites cause a skin irritation called mange. Some are contagious, like *Cheyletiella*, ear mites, scabies and chiggers. Mites that cause ear-mite infestations are usually controlled with Lindane, which can only be administered by a vet, followed by Tresaderm at home.

It is essential that your dog be treated for mange as quickly as possible because some forms of mange are transmissible to people.

INTERNAL PARASITES

Most animals—fishes, birds and mammals, including dogs and humans—have worms and other parasites that live inside their bodies. According to Dr Herbert R Axelrod, the fish pathologist, there are two kinds of parasites: dumb and smart. The smart parasites live in peaceful cooperation with their hosts (symbiosis), while the dumb parasites kill their host. Most of the worm infections are relatively easy to control. If they are not controlled they weaken the host dog to the point that other medical problems occur, but they are not dumb parasites.

ROUNDWORMS

The roundworms that infect dogs are scientifically known as *Toxocara canis*. They live in the dog's intestines. The worms shed eggs continually. It has been estimated that a dog produces about 150 grammes of faeces every day. Each gramme of faeces averages 10,000–12,000 eggs of roundworms. There are no known areas in which dogs roam that do not contain roundworm eggs. The greatest danger of roundworms is that they infect people too! It is wise to have your dog tested regularly for roundworms.

Pigs also have roundworm infections that can be passed to humans and dogs. The typical roundworm parasite is called *Ascaris lumbricoides*.

PHOTO BY CAROLINA BIOLOGICAL SUPPLY/PHOTOTAKE

The roundworm, *Rhabditis*. The roundworm can infect both dogs and humans.

ROUNDWORM

Average size dogs can pass 1,360,000 roundworm eggs every day.

For example, if there were only 1 million dogs in the world, the world would be saturated with 1,300 metric tonnes of dog faeces.

These faeces would contain 15,000,000,000 roundworm eggs.

It's known that 7–31% of home gardens and children's play boxes in the US contain roundworm eggs.

Flushing dog's faeces down the toilet is not a safe practice because the usual sewage treatments do not destroy roundworm eggs.

Infected puppies start shedding roundworm eggs at 3 weeks of age. They can be infected by their mother's milk.

DEWORMING

Ridding your puppy of worms is VERY IMPORTANT because certain worms that puppies carry, such as tapeworms and roundworms, can infect humans.

Breeders initiate a deworming programme at or about four weeks of age. The routine is repeated every two or three weeks until the puppy is three months old. The breeder from whom you obtained your puppy should provide you with the complete details of the deworming programme.

Your veterinary surgeon can prescribe and monitor the programme of deworming for you. The usual programme is treating the puppy every 15–20 days until the puppy is positively worm free.

It is advised that you only treat your puppy with drugs that are recommended professionally.

HOOKWORMS

The worm *Ancylostoma caninum* is commonly called the dog hookworm. It is dangerous to humans and cats. It also has teeth by which it attaches itself to the intestines of the dog. It changes the site of its attachment about six times a day and the dog loses blood from each detachment, possibly causing iron-deficiency anaemia. Hookworms are easily purged from the dog with many medications. Milbemycin oxime, which also serves as a heartworm preventative in Collies, can be used for this purpose.

In Britain the 'temperate climate' hookworm (*Uncinaria stenocephala*) is rarely found in pet or show dogs, but can occur in hunting packs, racing Greyhounds and sheepdogs because the worms can be prevalent wherever dogs are exercised regularly on grassland.

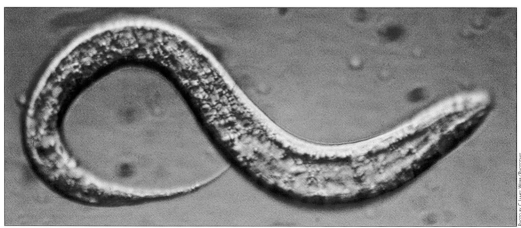

PHOTO BY C JAMES WEBB/PHOTOTAKE

The infective stage of the hookworm larva.

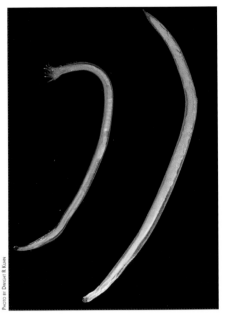

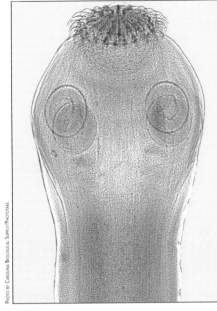

Left:
Male and female hookworms, *Ancylostoma caninum*, are uncommonly found in pet or show dogs in Britain. Hookworms may infect other dogs that have exposure to grasslands.

Right:
The head and rostellum (the round prominence on the scolex) of a tapeworm, which infects dogs and humans.

TAPEWORMS

There are many species of tapeworms. They are carried by fleas! The dog eats the flea and starts the tapeworm cycle. Humans can also be infected with tapeworms, so don't eat fleas! Fleas are so small that your dog could pass them onto your hands, your plate or your food and thus make it possible for you to ingest a flea which is carrying tapeworm eggs.

While tapeworm infection is not life threatening in dogs (smart parasite!), it can be the cause of a very serious liver disease for humans. About 50 percent of the humans infected with *Echinococcus multilocularis*, a type of tapeworm that causes alveolar hydatis, perish.

TAPEWORM

Humans, rats, squirrels, foxes, coyotes, wolves, mixed breeds of dogs and purebred dogs are all susceptible to tapeworm infection. Except in humans, tapeworms are usually not a fatal infection.

Infected individuals can harbour a thousand parasitic worms.

Tapeworms have two sexes—male and female (many other worms have only one sex—male and female in the same worm).

If dogs eat infected rats or mice, they get the tapeworm disease.

One month after attaching to a dog's intestine, the worm starts shedding eggs. These eggs are infective immediately.

Infective eggs can live for a few months without a host animal.

HEARTWORMS

Heartworms are thin, extended worms up to 30 cms (12 ins) long which live in a dog's heart and the major blood vessels surrounding it. Dogs may have up to 200 worms. Symptoms may be loss of energy, loss of appetite, coughing, the development of a pot belly and anaemia.

Heartworms are transmitted by mosquitoes. The mosquito drinks the blood of an infected dog and takes in larvae with the blood. The larvae, called microfilaria, develop within the body of the mosquito and are passed on to the next dog bitten after the larvae mature. It takes two to three weeks for the larvae to develop to the infective stage within the body of the mosquito. Dogs should be treated at about six weeks of age, and maintained on a prophylactic dose given monthly.

Blood testing for heartworms is not necessarily indicative of how seriously your dog is infected. This is a dangerous disease. Although heartworm is a problem for dogs in America, Australia, Asia and Central Europe, dogs in the United Kingdom are not currently affected by heartworm.

The heart of a dog infected with canine heartworm, *Dirofilaria immitis*.

PHOTO BY JAMES E HAYDEN, RPB/PHOTOTAKE

First Aid at a Glance

Burns
Place the affected area under cool water; use ice if only a small area is burnt.

Bee/Insect bites
Apply ice to relieve swelling; antihistamine dosed properly.

Animal bites
Clean any bleeding area; apply pressure until bleeding subsides; go to the vet.

Spider bites
Use cold compress and a pressurised pack to inhibit venom's spreading.

Antifreeze poisoning
Induce vomiting with hydrogen peroxide. Seek *immediate* veterinary help!

Fish hooks
Removal best handled by vet; hook must be cut in order to remove.

Snake bites
Pack ice around bite; contact vet quickly; identify snake for proper antivenin.

Car accident
Move dog from roadway with blanket; seek veterinary aid.

Shock
Calm the dog, keep him warm; seek immediate veterinary help.

Nosebleed
Apply cold compress to the nose; apply pressure to any visible abrasion.

Bleeding
Apply pressure above the area; treat wound by applying a cotton pack.

Heat stroke
Submerge dog in cold bath; cool down with fresh air and water; go to the vet.

Frostbite/Hypothermia
Warm the dog with a warm bath, electric blankets or hot water bottles.

Abrasions
Clean the wound and wash out thoroughly with fresh water; apply antiseptic.

 Remember: an injured dog may attempt to bite a helping hand from fear and confusion. Always muzzle the dog before trying to offer assistance.

HOMEOPATHY:
an alternative to conventional medicine

'Less is Most'

Using this principle, the strength of a homeopathic remedy is measured by the number of serial dilutions that were undertaken to create it. The greater the number of serial dilutions, the greater the strength of the homeopathic remedy. The potency of a remedy that has been made by making a dilution of 1 part in 100 parts (or 1/100) is 1c or 1cH. If this remedy is subjected to a series of further dilutions, each one being 1/100, a more dilute and stronger remedy is produced. If the remedy is diluted in this way six times, it is called 6c or 6cH. A dilution of 6c is 1 part in 1000,000,000,000. In general, higher potencies in more frequent doses are better for acute symptoms and lower potencies in more infrequent doses are more useful for chronic, long-standing problems.

CURING OUR DOGS NATURALLY

Holistic medicine means treating the whole animal as a unique, perfect living being. Generally, holistic treatments do not suppress the symptoms that the body naturally produces, as do most medications prescribed by conventional doctors and vets. Holistic methods seek to cure disease by regaining balance and harmony in the patient's environment. Some of these methods include use of nutritional therapy, herbs, flower essences, aromatherapy, acupuncture, massage, chiropractic, and, of course, the most popular holistic approach, homeopathy. Homeopathy is a theory or system of treating illness with small doses of substances which, if administered in larger quantities, would produce the symptoms that the patient already has. This approach is often described as 'like cures like.' Although modern veterinary medicine is geared toward the 'quick fix,' homeopathy relies on the belief that, given the time, the body is able to heal itself and return to its natural, healthy state.

Choosing a remedy to cure a problem in our dogs is the difficult part of homeopathy. Consult with your veterinary surgeon for a professional diagnosis of your dog's symptoms. Often these symptoms require immediate conventional

care. If your vet is willing, and somewhat knowledgeable, you may attempt a homeopathic remedy. Be aware that cortisone prevents homeopathic remedies from working. There are hundreds of possibilities and combinations to cure many problems in dogs, from basic physical problems such as excessive moulting, fleas or other parasites, unattractive doggy odour, bad breath, upset tummy, dry, oily or dull coat, diarrhoea, ear problems or eye discharge (including tears and dry or mucousy matter), to behavioural abnormalities, such as fear of loud noises, habitual licking, poor appetite, excessive barking, obesity and various phobias. From alumina to zincum metallicum, the remedies span the planet and the imagination…from flowers and weeds to chemicals, insect droppings, diesel smoke and volcanic ash.

Using 'Like to Treat Like'

Unlike conventional medicines that suppress symptoms, homeopathic remedies treat illnesses with small doses of substances that, if administered in larger quantities, would produce the symptoms that the patient already has. While the same homeopathic remedy can be used to treat different symptoms in different dogs, here are some interesting remedies and their uses.

Apis Mellifica
(made from honey bee venom) can be used for allergies or to reduce swelling that occurs in acutely infected kidneys.

Diesel Smoke
can be used to help control travel sickness.

Calcarea Fluorica
(made from calcium fluoride which helps harden bone structure) can be useful in treating hard lumps in tissues.

Natrum Muriaticum
(made from common salt, sodium chloride) is useful in treating thin, thirsty dogs.

Nitricum Acidum
(made from nitric acid) is used for symptoms you would expect to see from contact with acids such as lesions, especially where the skin joins the linings of body orifices or openings such as the lips and nostrils.

Symphytum
(made from the herb Knitbone, Symphytum officianale) is used to encourage bones to heal.

Urtica Urens
(made from the common stinging nettle) is used in treating painful, irritating rashes.

HOMEOPATHIC REMEDIES FOR YOUR DOG

Symptom/Ailment	Possible Remedy
ALLERGIES	Apis Mellifica 30c, Astacus Fluviatilis 6c, Pulsatilla 30c, Urtica Urens 6c
ALOPECIA	Alumina 30c, Lycopodium 30c, Sepia 30c, Thallium 6c
ANAL GLANDS (BLOCKED)	Hepar Sulphuris Calcareum 30c, Sanicula 6c, Silicea 6c
ARTHRITIS	Rhus Toxicodendron 6c, Bryonia Alba 6c
CATARACT	Calcarea Carbonica 6c, Conium Maculatum 6c, Phosphorus 30c, Silicea 30c
CONSTIPATION	Alumina 6c, Carbo Vegetabilis 30c, Graphites 6c, Nitricum Acidum 30c, Silicea 6c
COUGHING	Aconitum Napellus 6c, Belladonna 30c, Hyoscyamus Niger 30c, Phosphorus 30c
DIARRHOEA	Arsenicum Album 30c, Aconitum Napellus 6c, Chamomilla 30c, Mercurius Corrosivus 30c
DRY EYE	Zincum Metallicum 30c
EAR PROBLEMS	Aconitum Napellus 30c, Belladonna 30c, Hepar Sulphuris 30c, Tellurium 30c, Psorinum 200c
EYE PROBLEMS	Borax 6c, Aconitum Napellus 30c, Graphites 6c, Staphysagria 6c, Thuja Occidentalis 30c
GLAUCOMA	Aconitum Napellus 30c, Apis Mellifica 6c, Phosphorus 30c
HEAT STROKE	Belladonna 30c, Gelsemium Sempervirens 30c, Sulphur 30c
HICCOUGHS	Cinchona Deficinalis 6c
HIP DYSPLASIA	Colocynthis 6c, Rhus Toxicodendron 6c, Bryonia Alba 6c
INCONTINENCE	Argentum Nitricum 6c, Causticum 30c, Conium Maculatum 30c, Pulsatilla 30c, Sepia 30c
INSECT BITES	Apis Mellifica 30c, Cantharis 30c, Hypericum Perforatum 6c, Urtica Urens 30c
ITCHING	Alumina 30c, Arsenicum Album 30c, Carbo Vegetabilis 30c, Hypericum Perforatum 6c, Mezerium 6c, Sulphur 30c
KENNEL COUGH	Drosera 6c, Ipecacuanha 30c
MASTITIS	Apis Mellifica 30c, Belladonna 30c, Urtica Urens 1m
PATELLAR LUXATION	Gelsemium Sempervirens 6c, Rhus Toxicodendron 6c
PENIS PROBLEMS	Aconitum Napellus 30c, Hepar Sulphuris Calcareum 30c, Pulsatilla 30c, Thuja Occidentalis 6c
PUPPY TEETHING	Calcarea Carbonica 6c, Chamomilla 6c, Phytolacca 6c
TRAVEL SICKNESS	Cocculus 6c, Petroleum 6c

Recognising a Sick Dog

Unlike colicky babies and cranky children, our canine kids cannot tell us when they are feeling ill. Therefore, there are a number of signs that owners can identify to know that their dogs are not feeling well.

Take note for physical manifestations such as:

- unusual, bad odour, including bad breath
- excessive moulting
- wax in the ears, chronic ear irritation
- oily, flaky, dull haircoat
- mucous, tearing or similar discharge in the eyes
- fleas or mites
- mucous in stool, diarrhoea
- sensitivity to petting or handling
- licking at paws, scratching face, etc.

Keep an eye out for behavioural changes as well including:

- lethargy, idleness
- lack of patience or general irritability
- lack of appetite, digestive problems
- phobias (fear of people, loud noises, etc.)
- strange behaviour, suspicion, fear
- coprophagia
- more frequent barking
- whimpering, crying

Get Well Soon

You don't need a DVR or a BVMA to provide good TLC to your sick or recovering dog, but you do need to pay attention to some details that normally wouldn't bother him. The following tips will aid Fido's recovery and get him back on his paws again:

- Keep his space free of irritating smells, like heavy perfumes and air fresheners.
- Rest is the best medicine! Avoid harsh lighting that will prevent your dog from sleeping. Shade him from bright sunlight during the day and dim the lights in the evening.
- Keep the noise level down. Animals are more sensitive to sound when they are sick.

- Be attentive to any necessary temperature adjustments. A dog with a fever needs a cool room and cold liquids. A bitch that is whelping or recovering from surgery will be more comfortable in a warm room, consuming warm liquids and food.
- You wouldn't send a sick child back to school early, so don't rush your dog back into a full routine until he seems absolutely ready.

A Puli should have clear, healthy eyes.

A PET OWNER'S GUIDE TO COMMON OPHTHALMIC DISEASES
by Prof. Dr Robert L Peiffer, Jr.

Few would argue that vision is the most important of the cognitive senses, and maintenance of a normal visual system is important for an optimal quality of life. Likewise, pet owners tend to be acutely aware of their pet's eyes and vision, which is important because early detection of ocular disease will optimize therapeutic outcomes. The eye is a sensitive organ with minimal reparative capabilities, and with some diseases, such as glaucoma, uveitis and retinal detachment, delay in diagnosis and treatment can be critical in terms of whether vision can be preserved.

Lower entropion, or rolling in of the eyelid, is causing irritation in the left eye of this young dog. Several extra eyelashes, or distichiasis, are present on the upper lid.

The causes of ocular disease are quite varied; the nature of dogs make them susceptible to traumatic conditions, the most common of which include proptosis of the globe, cat scratch injuries and penetrating wounds from foreign objects, including sticks and air rifle pellets. Infectious diseases caused by bacteria, viruses or fungi may be localized to the eye or part of a systemic infection. Many of the common conditions, including eyelid conformational problems, cataracts, glaucoma and retinal degenerations have a genetic basis.

Before acquiring your puppy it is important to ascertain that both parents have been examined and certified free of eye disease by a veterinary ophthalmologist. Since many of these genetic diseases can be detected early in life, acquire the pup with the condition that it pass a thorough ophthalmic examination by a qualified specialist.

LID CONFORMATIONAL ABNORMALITIES
Rolling in (entropion) or out (ectropion) of the lids tends to be a breed-related problem. Entropion can involve the upper and/or lower lids. Signs usually appear between 3 and 12 months of age. The irritation caused by the eyelid hairs rubbing

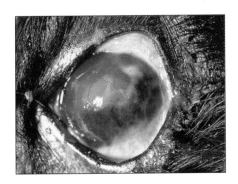

on the surface of the cornea may result in blinking, tearing and damage to the cornea. Ectropion is likewise breed-related and is considered 'normal' in hounds, for instance; unlike entropion, which results in acute discomfort, ectropion may cause chronic irritation related to exposure and the pooling of secretions. Most of these cases can be managed medically with daily irrigation with sterile saline and topical antibiotics when required.

EYELASH ABNORMALITIES
Dogs normally have lashes only on the upper lids, in contrast to humans. Occasionally, extra eyelashes may be seen emerging at the eyelid margin (distichiasis) or through the inner surface of the eyelid (ectopic cilia).

CONJUNCTIVITIS
Inflammation of the conjunctiva, the pink tissue that lines the lids and the anterior portion of the sclera, is generally accompanied by redness, discharge and mild discomfort. The majority of cases are either associated with bacterial infections or dry eye syndrome. Fortunately, topical medications are generally effective in curing or controlling the problem.

DRY EYE SYNDROME
Dry eye syndrome (keratoconjunctivitis sicca) is a common cause of external ocular disease. Discharge is typically thick and sticky, and keratitis is a frequent component; any breed can be affected. While some cases can be associated with toxic effects of drugs, including the sulfa antibiotics, the cause in the majority of the cases cannot be determined and is assumed to be immune-mediated.

Keratoconjunctivitis sicca, seen here in the right eye of a middle-aged dog, causes a characteristic thick mucous discharge as well as secondary corneal changes.

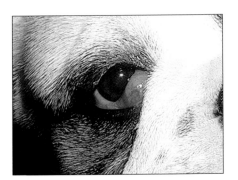

Left: Prolapse of the gland of the third eyelid in the right eye of a pup. Right: In this case, in the right eye of a young dog, the prolapsed gland can be seen emerging between the edge of the third eyelid and the corneal surface.

Multiple deep ulcerations affect the cornea of this middle-aged dog.

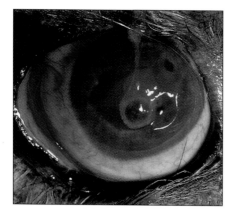

PROLAPSE OF THE GLAND OF THE THIRD EYELID

In this condition, commonly referred to as *cherry eye*, the gland of the third eyelid, which produces about one-third of the aqueous phase of the tear film and is normally situated within the anterior orbit, prolapses to emerge as a pink fleshy mass protruding over the edge of the third eyelid, between the third eyelid and the cornea. The condition usually develops during the first year of life and, while mild irritation may result, the condition is unsightly as much as anything else.

Lipid deposition can occur as a primary inherited dystrophy, or secondarily to hypercholesterolemia (in dogs frequently associated with hypothyroidism), chronic corneal inflammation or neoplasia. The deposits in this dog assume an oval pattern in the centre of the cornea.

CORNEAL DISEASE

The cornea is the clear front part of the eye that provides the first step in the collection of light on its journey to be eventually focused onto the retina, and most corneal diseases will be manifested by alterations in corneal transparency. The cornea is an exquisitely innervated tissue, and defects in corneal integrity are accompanied by pain, which is demonstrated by squinting.

Corneal ulcers may occur secondary to trauma or to irritation from entropion or ectopic cilia. In middle-aged or older dogs, epithelial ulcerations may occur spontaneously due to an inherent defect; these are referred to as indolent or Boxer ulcers, in recognition of the breed in which we see the condition most frequently. Infection may occur secondarily. Ulcers can be potentially blinding conditions; severity is dependent upon the size and depth of the ulcer and other complicating features.

Non-ulcerative keratitis tends to have an immune-mediated component and is managed by topical immunosuppressants, usually corticosteroids. Corneal edema can occur in elderly dogs. It is due to a failure of the corneal endothelial 'pump.'

The cornea responds to chronic irritation by transforming

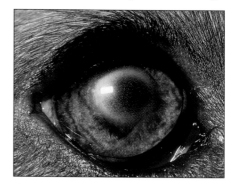

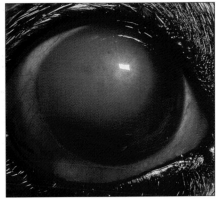

into skin-like tissue that is evident clinically by pigmentation, scarring and vascularization; some cases may respond to tear stimulants, lubricants and topical corticosteroids, while others benefit from surgical narrowing of the eyelid opening in order to enhance corneal protection.

UVEITIS

Inflammation of the vascular tissue of the eye–the uvea—is a common and potentially serious disease in dogs. While it may occur secondarily to trauma or other intraocular diseases, such as

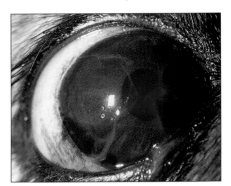

cataracts, most commonly uveitis is associated with some type of systemic infectious or neoplastic process. Uncontrolled, uveitis can lead to blinding cataracts, glaucoma and/or retinal detachments, and aggressive symptomatic therapy with dilating agents (to prevent pupillary adhesions) and anti-inflammatories are critical.

GLAUCOMA

The eye is essentially a hollow fluid-filled sphere, and the pressure within is maintained by regulation of the rate of fluid production and fluid egress at 10–20 mms of mercury. The retinal cells are extremely sensitive to elevations of intraocular pressure and, unless controlled, permanent blindness can occur within hours to days. In acute glaucoma, the conjunctiva becomes congested, the cornea cloudy, the pupil moderate and fixed; the eye is generally painful and avisual. Increased constant signs of

Corneal edema can develop as a slowly progressive process in elderly Boston Terriers, Miniature Dachshunds and Miniature Poodles, as well as others, as a result of the inability of the corneal endothelial 'pump' to maintain a state of dehydration.

Medial pigmentary keratitis in this dog is associated with irritation from prominent facial folds.

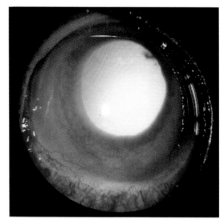

Glaucoma in the dog most commonly occurs as a sudden extreme elevation of intraocular pressure, frequently to three to four times the norm. The eye of this dog demonstrates the common signs of episcleral injection, or redness; mild diffuse corneal cloudiness, due to edema; and a mid-sized fixed pupil.

discomfort will accompany chronic cases.

Management of glaucoma is one of the most challenging situations the veterinary ophthalmologist faces; in spite of intense efforts, many of these cases will result in blindness.

Cataracts and Lens Dislocation

Cataracts are the most common blinding condition in dogs; fortunately, they are readily amenable to surgical intervention, with excellent results in terms of restoration of vision and replace-

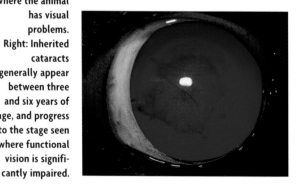

Left: The typical posterior subcapsular cataract appears between one and two years of age, but rarely progresses to where the animal has visual problems. Right: Inherited cataracts generally appear between three and six years of age, and progress to the stage seen where functional vision is significantly impaired.

ment of the cataractous lens with a synthetic one. Most cataracts in dogs are inherited; less commonly cataracts can be secondary to trauma, other ocular diseases, including uveitis, glaucoma, lens luxation and retinal degeneration, or secondary to an underlying systemic metabolic disease, including diabetes and Cushing's disease. Signs include a progressive loss of the bright dark appearance of the pupil, which is replaced by a blue-grey hazy appearance. In this respect, cataracts need to be distinguished from the normal ageing process of nuclear sclerosis, which occurs in middle-aged or older animals, and has minimal effect on vision.

Lens dislocation occurs in dogs and frequently leads to secondary glaucoma; early removal of the dislocated lens is generally curative.

Retinal Disease

Retinal degenerations are usually inherited, but may be associated with vitamin E deficiency in dogs.

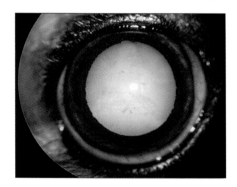

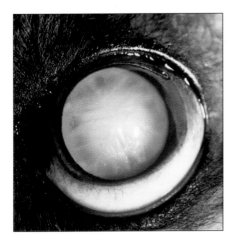

While signs are variable, most frequently one notes a decrease in vision over a period of months, which typically starts out as a night blindness. The cause of a more rapid loss of vision due to retinal degeneration occurs over days to weeks is labeled sudden acquired retinal degeneration or SARD; the outcome, however, is unfortunately usually similar to inherited and nutritional conditions, as the retinal tissues possess minimal regenerative capabilities. Most pets, however, with a bit of extra care and attention, show an amazing ability to adapt to an avisual world, and can be maintained as pets with a satisfactory quality of life. Detachment of the retina—due to accumulation of blood between the retina and the underling uvea, which is called the *choroid*—can occur secondarily to retinal tears or holes, tractional forces within the eye, or as a result of uveitis. These types of detachments may be amenable to surgical repair if diagnosed early.

OPTIC NERVE

Optic neuritis, or inflammation of the nerve that connects the eye with the brain stem, is a relatively uncommon condition that presents usually with rather sudden loss of vision and widely dilated non-responsive pupils.

Anterior lens luxation can occur as a primary disease in the terrier breeds, or secondarily to trauma. The fibres that hold the lens in place rupture and the lens may migrate through the pupil to be situated in front of the iris. Secondary glaucoma is a frequent and significant complication that can be avoided if the dislocated lens is removed surgically.

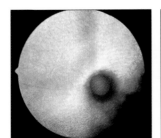 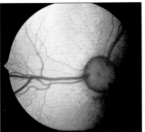 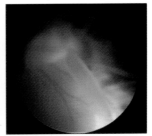 

Left: The posterior pole of a normal fundus is shown; prominent are the head of the optic nerve and the retinal blood vessels. The retina is transparent, and the prominent green tapetum is seen superiorly.
Centre: An eye with inherited retinal dysplasia is depicted. The tapetal retina superior to the optic disc is disorganised, with multifocal areas of hyperplasia of the retinal pigment epithelium.
Right: Severe collie eye anomaly and a retinal detachment; this eye is unfortunately blind.

Number-One Killer Disease in Dogs: CANCER

In every age there is a word associated with a disease or plague that causes humans to shudder. In the 21st century, that word is 'cancer.' Just as cancer is the leading cause of death in humans, it claims nearly half the lives of dogs that die from a natural disease as well as half the dogs that die over the age of ten years.

Described as a genetic disease, cancer becomes a greater risk as the dog ages. Veterinary surgeons and dog owners have become increasingly aware of the threat of cancer to dogs. Statistics reveal that one dog in every five will develop cancer, the most common of which is skin cancer. Many cancers, including prostate, ovarian and breast cancer, can be avoided by spaying and neutering our dogs by the age of six months.

Early detection of cancer can save or extend your dog's life, so it is absolutely vital for owners to have their dogs examined by a qualified veterinary surgeon or oncologist immediately upon detection of any abnormality. Certain dietary guidelines have also proven to reduce the onset and spread of cancer. Foods based on fish rather than beef, due to the presence of Omega-3 fatty acids, are recommended. Other amino acids such as glutamine have significant benefits for canines, particularly those breeds that show a greater susceptibility to cancer.

Cancer management and treatments promise hope for future generations of canines. Since the disease is genetic, breeders should never breed a dog whose parents, grandparents and any related siblings have developed cancer. It is difficult to know whether to exclude an otherwise healthy dog from a breeding programme as the disease does not manifest itself until the dog's senior years.

RECOGNISE CANCER WARNING SIGNS

Since early detection can possibly rescue your dog from becoming a cancer statistic, it is essential for owners to recognise the possible signs and seek the assistance of a qualified professional.

- Abnormal bumps or lumps that continue to grow
- Bleeding or discharge from any body cavity
- Persistent stiffness or lameness
- Recurrent sores or sores that do not heal
- Inappetence
- Breathing difficulties
- Weight loss
- Bad breath or odours
- General malaise and fatigue
- Eating and swallowing problems
- Difficulty urinating and defecating

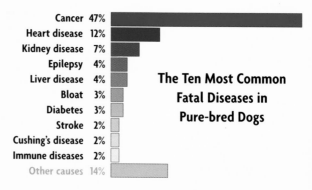

Cancer 47%
Heart disease 12%
Kidney disease 7%
Epilepsy 4%
Liver disease 4%
Bloat 3%
Diabetes 3%
Stroke 2%
Cushing's disease 2%
Immune diseases 2%
Other causes 14%

The Ten Most Common Fatal Diseases in Pure-bred Dogs

CDS: COGNITIVE DYSFUNCTION SYNDROME
'OLD DOG SYNDROME'

There are many ways for you to evaluate old-dog syndrome. Veterinary surgeons have defined CDS (cognitive dysfunction syndrome) as the gradual deterioration of cognitive abilities. These are indicated by changes in the dog's behaviour. When a dog changes its routine response, and maladies have been eliminated as the cause of these behavioural changes, then CDS is the usual diagnosis.

More than half the dogs over 8 years old suffer some form of CDS. The older the dog, the more chance it has of suffering from CDS. In humans, doctors often dismiss the CDS behavioural changes as part of 'winding down.'

There are four major signs of CDS: frequent toilet accidents inside the home, sleeps much more or much less than normal, acts confused, and fails to respond to social stimuli.

SYMPTOMS OF CDS

FREQUENT TOILET ACCIDENTS
- Urinates in the house.
- Defecates in the house.
- Doesn't signal that he wants to go out.

SLEEP PATTERNS
- Moves much more slowly.
- Sleeps more than normal during the day.
- Sleeps less during the night.

CONFUSION
- Goes outside and just stands there.
- Appears confused with a faraway look in his eyes.
- Hides more often.
- Doesn't recognise friends.
- Doesn't come when called.
- Walks around listlessly and without a destination goal.

FAILS TO RESPOND TO SOCIAL STIMULI
- Comes to people less frequently, whether called or not.
- Doesn't tolerate petting for more than a short time.
- Doesn't come to the door when you return home from work.

Your Senior
HUNGARIAN PULI

The Puli is well known for its longevity, and dogs living into their mid-teens are quite normal in the breed. Providing a sensible diet and exercise routine ensures that your Puli will enjoy the longevity of his forefathers. If dogs are over-indulged and allowed to become obese, they will in turn become reluctant to take exercise, which ultimately can shorten their lifespan. We have been fortunate, having had veterans (over seven years of age) who behave and look like youngsters.

Few breeds compare to the longevity of the Puli, save those long-lived tykes in the Toy Group! It is not uncommon to meet a senior Chihuahua in his late teens. On the other hand, one frequently meets large-breed owners who have had the sad task of saying good-bye to their Bullmastiffs or Great Danes at the young age of six or seven. If people live to be 100 years old, dogs live to be 20 years old. While this is a good rule of thumb, it is very inaccurate. When trying to compare dog years to human years, you cannot make a generalisation about all dogs. Dogs are generally considered mature within three years, but they can reproduce even earlier. So the first three years of a dog's life are like seven times that of comparable humans. That means a 3-year-old dog is like a 21-year-old human. As the curve of comparison shows, there is no hard and fast rule for comparing dog and

GETTING OLD

The bottom line is simply that a dog is getting old when YOU think it is getting old because it slows down in its general activities, including walking, running, eating, jumping and retrieving. On the other hand, certain activities increase, such as more sleeping, more barking and more repetition of habits like going to the door without being called when you put your coat on to leave or go outdoors.

human ages. The comparison is made even more difficult, for not all humans age at the same rate...and human females live longer than human males.

WHAT TO LOOK FOR IN SENIORS

Most veterinary surgeons and behaviourists use the seventh year mark as the time to consider a dog a 'senior.' The term 'senior' does not imply that the dog is geriatric and has begun to fail in mind and body. Ageing is essentially a slowing process. Humans readily admit that they feel a difference in

CONSISTENCY COUNTS

Puppies and older dogs are very similar in their need for consistency in their lives. Older pets may experience hearing and vision loss, or may just be more easily confused by changes in their homes. Try not to change the feeding schedule or the diet. Doors that are always open or closed should remain so. Most importantly, don't dismiss a pet just because he's getting old; most remain active and important parts of their owners' lives.

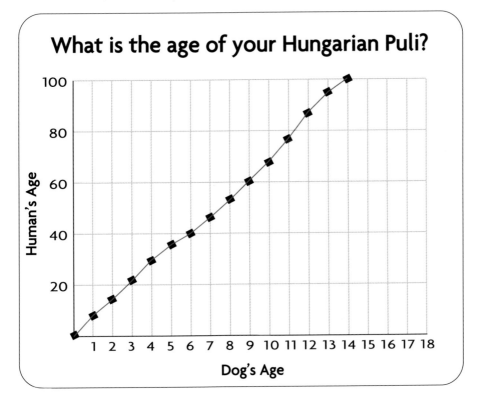

What is the age of your Hungarian Puli?
(Human's Age vs Dog's Age)

NOTICING THE SYMPTOMS

The symptoms listed below are symptoms that gradually appear and become more noticeable. They are not life threatening; however, the symptoms below are to be taken very seriously and a discussion with your veterinary surgeon is warranted:

• Your dog cries and whimpers when it moves and stops running completely.

• Convulsions start or become more serious and frequent. The usual convulsion (spasm) is when the dog stiffens and starts to tremble being unable or unwilling to move. The seizure usually lasts for 5 to 30 minutes.

• Your dog drinks more water and urinates more frequently. Wetting and bowel accidents take place indoors without warning.

• Vomiting becomes more and more frequent.

their activity level from age 20 to 30, and then from 30 to 40, etc. By treating the seven-year-old dog as a senior, owners are able to implement certain therapeutic and preventative medical strategies with the help of their veterinary surgeons. A senior-care programme should include at least two veterinary visits per year, screening sessions to determine the dog's health status, as well as nutritional counselling. Veterinary surgeons determine the senior dog's health status through a blood smear for a complete blood count, serum chemistry profile with electrolytes, urinalysis, blood pressure check, electrocardiogram, ocular tonometry (pressure on the eyeball) and dental prophylaxis.

Such an extensive programme for senior dogs is well advised before owners start to see the obvious physical signs of ageing, such as slower and inhibited movement, greying, increased sleep/nap periods and disinterest in play and other activity. This preventative programme promises a longer, healthier life for the ageing dog. Among the physical problems common in ageing dogs are the loss of sight and hearing, arthritis, kidney and liver failure, diabetes mellitus, heart disease, and Cushing's disease (a hormonal disease).

In addition to the physical manifestations discussed, there

are some behavioural changes and problems related to ageing dogs. Dogs suffering from hearing or vision loss, dental discomfort or arthritis can become aggressive. Likewise the near-deaf and/or blind dog may be startled more easily and react in an unexpectedly aggressive manner. Seniors suffering from senility can become more impatient and irritable. Housesoiling accidents are associated with loss of mobility, kidney problems, loss of sphincter control as well as plaque accumulation, physiological brain changes and reactions to medications. Older dogs, just like young puppies, suffer from separation anxiety, which can lead to excessive barking, whining, housesoiling and destructive behaviour. Seniors may become fearful of everyday sounds, such as vacuum cleaners, heaters, thunder and passing traffic. Some dogs have difficulty sleeping, due to discomfort, the need for frequent toilet visits and the like.

Owners should avoid spoiling the older dog with too many fatty treats. Obesity is a common problem in older dogs and subtracts years from their lifespan. Keep the senior dog as trim as possible since excessive weight puts additional stress on the body's vital organs. Some breeders recommend supplementing the diet with foods high in fibre and lower in calories. Adding fresh

SENIOR SIGNS

An old dog starts to show one or more of the following symptoms:

• The hair on its face and paws starts to turn grey. The colour breakdown usually starts around the eyes and mouth.

• Sleep patterns are deeper and longer and the old dog is harder to awaken.

• Food intake diminishes.

• Responses to calls, whistles and other signals are ignored more and more.

• Eye contacts do not evoke tail wagging (assuming they once did).

TO THE RESCUE
Some people choose to adopt or 'rescue' older dogs instead of buying a new puppy. Older dogs may have come from abusive environments and be fearful, and some dogs have just developed many bad habits, which can present a challenge to their new owners. Training an older dog will take more time and patience, but persistence and an abundance of praise and love can transform a dog into a well-behaved, loyal companion.

AGEING ADDITIVES
A healthy diet is important for dogs of all ages, but older dogs may benefit from the addition of supplements like antioxidants, which fight the ageing process, and vitamin B, which aids the kidneys. Check with your vet before adding these to your pet's diet.

vegetables and marrow broth to the senior's diet makes a tasty, low-calorie, low-fat supplement. Vets also offer speciality diets for senior dogs that are worth exploring.

Your dog, as he nears his twilight years, needs his owner's patience and good care more than ever. Never punish an older dog for an accident or abnormal behaviour. For all the years of love, protection and companionship that your dog has provided, he deserves special attention and courtesies. The older dog may need to relieve himself at 3 a.m. because he can no longer hold it for eight hours. Older dogs may not be able to remain crated for more than two or three hours. It may be time to give up a sofa or chair to your old friend. Although he may not seem as enthusiastic

about your attention and petting, he does appreciate the considerations you offer as he gets older.

Your Puli does not understand why his world is slowing down. Owners must make the transition into the golden years as pleasant and rewarding as possible.

WHEN THE TIME COMES
You are never fully prepared to make a rational decision about putting your dog to sleep. It is very obvious that you love your Puli or you would not be reading this book. Putting a loved dog to

KEEPING SENIORS WARM
The coats of many older dogs become thinner as they age, which makes them more susceptible to cold and illness. During cold weather, limit time spent outdoors, and be extremely cautious with any artificial sources of warmth such as heat lamps, as these can cause severe burns. Your oldtimer may need a sweater to wear over his coat.

sleep is extremely difficult. It is a decision that must be made with your veterinary surgeon. You are usually forced to make the decision when one of the life-threatening symptoms listed above becomes serious enough for you to seek medical (veterinary) help.

If the prognosis of the malady indicates the end is near and your beloved pet will only suffer more and experience no enjoyment for the balance of its life, then euthanasia is the right choice.

WHAT IS EUTHANASIA?
Euthanasia derives from the Greek meaning good death. In other words, it means the planned, painless killing of a dog suffering from a painful, incurable condition, or who is so aged that it cannot walk, see, eat or control its excretory functions.

Euthanasia is usually accomplished by injection with an overdose of an anaesthesia or barbiturate. Aside from the prick of the needle, the experience is usually painless.

Owners often have the option of memorialising their beloved pets in pet cemeteries.

MAKING THE DECISION
The decision to euthanise your dog is never easy. The days during which the dog becomes ill and the end occurs can be unusually stressful for you. If this is your first experience with the death of a loved one, you may need the comfort dictated by your religious beliefs. If you are the head of the family and have children, you should have involved them in the decision of putting your Puli to sleep. Usually your dog can be maintained on drugs for a few

> **EUTHANASIA**
> Euthanasia must be done by a licensed veterinary surgeon. There also may be societies for the prevention of cruelty to animals in your area. They often offer this service upon a vet's recommendation.

COPING WITH LOSS

When your dog dies, you may be as upset as when a human companion passes away. You are losing your protector, your baby, your confidante and best friend. Many people experience not only grief but also feelings of guilt and doubt as to whether they did all that they could for their pet. Allow yourself to grieve and mourn, and seek help from friends and support groups. You may also wish to consult books and websites that deal with this topic.

days in order to give you ample time to make a decision. During this time, talking with members of your family or even people who have lived through this same experience can ease the burden of your inevitable decision.

THE FINAL RESTING PLACE

Dogs can have some of the same privileges as humans. The remains of your beloved dog can be buried in a pet cemetery, which is generally expensive. Dogs who have died at home can be buried in your garden in a place suitably marked with some stone or newly planted tree or bush. Alternatively, they can be cremated individually and the ashes returned to you. A less expensive option is mass cremation, although, of course, the ashes can not then be returned. Vets can usually arrange

Many cities have pet cemeteries conveniently located. Your veterinary surgeon can assist you in locating one.

the cremation on your behalf. The cost of these options should always be discussed frankly and openly with your veterinary surgeon. In Britain if your dog has died at the surgery the vet legally cannot allow you to take your dog's body home.

GETTING ANOTHER DOG?

The grief of losing your beloved dog will be as lasting as the grief

> **AN ANCIENT ACHE**
>
> As ancient a disease as any, arthritis remains poorly explained for human and dog alike. Fossils dating back 100 million years show the deterioration of arthritis. Human fossils two millions years old show the disease in man. The most common type of arthritis affecting dogs is known as osteoarthritis, which sets in adult dogs before their senior years. Obesity aggravating the dog's joints has been cited as a factor in arthritis.
>
> Rheumatoid disease destroys joint cartilage and causes arthritic joints. Pituitary dysfunctions as well as diabetes have been associated with arthritis. Veterinary surgeons treat arthritis variously, including aspirin, 'bed rest' in the dog's crate, physical therapy and exercise, heat therapy (with a heating pad), providing soft bedding materials, and corticosteroids (to reduce pain and swelling temporarily). Your vet will be able to recommend a course of action to help relieve your arthritic chum.

of losing a human friend or relative. In most cases, if your dog died of old age (if there is such a thing), it had slowed down considerably. Do you want a new Puli puppy to replace it? Or are you better off finding a more mature Puli, say two to three years of age, which will usually be housetrained and will have an already developed personality. In this case, you can find out if you like each other after a few hours of being together.

The decision is, of course, your own. Do you want another Puli or perhaps a different breed so as to avoid comparison with your beloved friend? Most people usually buy the same breed because they know (and love) the characteristics of that breed. Then, too, they often know people who have the same breed and perhaps they are lucky enough that one of their friends expects a litter soon. What could be better?

In most pet cemeteries there are special areas in which your dog's ashes can be stored. The urns are usually available at the crematorium.

Showing Your
PULI

When you purchased your Puli you will have made it clear to the breeder whether you wanted one just as a loveable companion and pet, or if you hoped to be buying a Puli with show prospects. No reputable breeder will have sold you a young puppy saying that it was definitely of show quality for so much can go wrong during the early months of a puppy's development. If you plan to show, what you will hopefully have acquired is a puppy with 'show potential.'

SHOW PREPARATION

Should you decide that you might try showing your Puli, then preparation cannot start too early. Accustom the youngster to standing on a table as soon as possible so he will not be surprised to be put up on a table for something other than a veterinary examination. Just a few minutes getting the dog used to having someone putting his hands over the body, looking at the teeth, etc., are sufficient to begin. Training classes are a great help for your future show dog so that he will come to accept the approaches and handling of strangers. Talk to your Puli while he is on the table, so that by the

tone of your voice he feels reassured. It's very unfair to both the dog and the judge if the latter is expected to evaluate an upset animal, and you blame the dog for reacting to a totally unfamiliar experience. It's important that your Puli get used to having his dentition inspected, for a judge will wish to see that the teeth are correctly positioned and in good condition and that the jaw closes properly. In the Puli, dogs not only need to have their teeth checked but must have the roof of

INFORMATION ON CLUBS

You can get information about dog shows from kennel clubs and breed clubs:

Fédération Cynologique Internationale
14, rue Leopold II, B-6530 Thuin, Belgium
www.fci.be

The Kennel Club
1-5 Clarges St., Piccadilly, London W1Y 8AB, UK
www.the-kennel-club.org.uk

American Kennel Club
5580 Centerview Dr., Raleigh, NC 27606-3390, USA
www.akc.org

Canadian Kennel Club
89 Skyway Ave., Suite 100, Etobicoke, Ontario M9W 6R4 Canada
www.ckc.ca

SHOW QUALITY SHOWS

While you may purchase a puppy in the hope of having a successful career in the show ring, it is impossible to tell, at eight to ten weeks, whether your dog will be a contender. Some promising pups end up with minor to serious faults that prevent them from taking home a Best of Breed award, but this certainly does not mean they can't be the best of companions for you and your family. To find out if your potential show dog is show quality, enter him in a match to see how a judge evaluates him. You may also take him back to your breeder as he matures to see what he might advise.

trotting alongside his handler on a loose lead, in order to show off his natural, light and springy action. There is no call to 'string' the Puli up on a tight lead like a terrier. A tight lead will also cause the neck to be stretched in an unnatural manner and angle and will affect the dog's natural action.

Preparation for show is not only ring training but also the coat and its presentation. The Kennel Club is likely to test coats of show dogs for the use of artifice in presentation, therefore if something like oil or lacquer has been used, it will soon be identified. Most owners will use some condition, perhaps in the form of lanolin, to prevent the cords from

the mouth inspected as well, since the standard requires a pigmented mouth.

Though the standard calls for a wiry dog in hard working condition, this must be checked by a 'hands-on' examination for construction, muscle tone, etc. Puppies must become accustomed to having a stranger feel their bones, spring of rib, loin, tail and other points. With the legs, the judge needs to get under the cords to find a good bend of stifle at the rear and a strong hock joint that does not flex forward.

The puppy must be trained to a lead so that its gait can be evaluated in the show ring. When the Puli is moved, it is best seen

The author, Ann Arch, handling a young puppy bitch.

The author's daughter, Alex Davis, and her Puli, winning a Challenge Certificate.

very wet dog! We use old towels to absorb as much of the water as possible, before using the dryer. The more water that can be wrung out, the quicker the drying time. The best time to work thoroughly through the whole coat is when the dog is practically dry, ensuring that all cords are separated right down to the skin level.

In our show dogs with full mature cords, we find it easiest to keep them from getting too dirty by looping the cords into bundles so that they are carried well above the ground and are less likely to become soiled or pick up debris. The bands used to hold the bundles should not be too tight or they will cut through the hair. We prefer the terry-towel type that are strong but gentle. Pre-show bathing varies from one dog and its coat type to the next. Some

drying out too much. These preparations must be removed by careful bathing and rinsing before exhibiting. We normally trim around the feet to neaten them and tidy up the long cords that reach down on to the ground, so that the coat swings easily while moving. The cords of the tail, as naturally carried over the body, should merge with those of the body and hindlegs, so these tail cords may also need reducing in length if they become too long.

A thorough bath and complete rinsing to ensure that the coat is quite natural will leave you with a

WINNING THE TICKET

Earning a championship at Kennel Club shows is the most difficult in the world. Compared to the United States and Canada where it is relatively not 'challenging,' collecting three green tickets not only requires much time and effort, it can be very expensive! Challenge Certificates, as the tickets are properly known, are the building blocks of champions— good breeding, good handling, good training and good luck!

Pulik will need bathing several days before the show, while others can be bathed a day or so in advance.

UNDERSTANDING DOG SHOWS

To the novice, exhibiting a Puli in the show ring may look easy but it takes a lot of hard work, study and devotion to do top winning at a show such as the prestigious Crufts, not to mention a little luck too! Dog shows can be fun to watch and even more fun to participate in.

The first concept that the canine novice learns when watching a dog show is that each dog first competes against members of its own breed. Once the judge has selected the best member of each breed, provided that the show is judged on a Group system, that chosen dog will compete with other dogs in its group. Finally the best of each group will compete for Best in Show and Reserve Best in Show.

The second concept that you must understand is that the dogs are not actually competing against one another. The judge compares each dog against the breed standard, which is a written description of the ideal specimen of the breed. While some early breed standards were indeed based on specific dogs that were famous or popular, many dedicated enthusiasts say that a perfect specimen, described in the standard, has never walked into a show ring, has never been bred and, to the woe of dog breeders around the globe, does not exist. Breeders attempt to get as close to this ideal as possible, with every

If you intend to show your Puli, it should be trained to tolerate handling by a stranger. The judge uses his hands to evaluate the dog's structure and conformation to the breed standard.

litter, but theoretically the 'perfect' dog is so elusive that it is impossible. (And if the 'perfect' dog were born, breeders and judges would never agree that it was indeed 'perfect.')

If you are interested in exploring dog shows, your best bet is to join your local breed club. These clubs often host both Championship and Open Shows, and sometimes Match meetings and special events, all of which could be of interest, even if you are only an onlooker. Clubs also send out newsletters and some organise training days and seminars in order that people may learn more about their chosen breed. To locate the breed club closest to you, contact The Kennel

SEVEN GROUPS

The Kennel Club divides its dogs into seven Groups: Gundogs, Utility, Working, Toy, Terrier, Hounds and Pastoral.*

*The Pastoral Group, established in 1999, includes those sheepdog breeds previously categorised in the Working Group.

Club, the ruling body for the British dog world. The Kennel Club governs not only conformation shows but also working trials, agility trials and field trials. The Kennel Club furnishes the rules and regulations for all these events plus general dog registration and other basic requirements of dog ownership. Its annual

Author Ann Arch and daughter Alex Davis groom a Puli before showing.

Dog showing is not only about ribbons, medals and trophy cups. It is also about prestige and the rewarding feeling of owning a championship quality dog.

show, called the Crufts Dog Show, held in Birmingham, is the largest benched show in England. Every year over 20,000 of the UK's best dogs qualify to partici-

DID YOU KNOW?

The FCI *does not* issue pedigrees. The FCI members and contract partners are responsible for issuing pedigrees and training judges in their own countries. The FCI does maintain a list of judges and makes sure that they are recognised throughout the FCI member countries.

The FCI also *does not* act as a breeder referral; breeder information is available from FCI-recognised national canine societies in each of the FCI's member countries.

pate in this marvellous show which lasts four days.

The Kennel Club governs many different kinds of shows in Great Britain, Australia, South Africa and beyond. At the most competitive and prestigious of these shows, the Championship Shows, a dog can earn Challenge Certificates (CCs), and thereby become a Show Champion or a Champion. A dog must earn three Challenge Certificates under three different judges to earn the prefix of 'Sh Ch' or 'Ch.' Note that some breeds must also qualify in a field trial in order to gain the title of full champion. Challenge Certificates are awarded to a very small percentage of the dogs competing, and dogs that are already

HOW TO ENTER A DOG SHOW

1. Obtain an entry form and show schedule from the Show Secretary.
2. Select the classes that you want to enter and complete the entry form.
3. Transfer your dog into your name at The Kennel Club. (Be sure that this matter is handled before entering.)
4. Find out how far in advance show entries must be made. Often it's more than a couple of months.

the groups; and a Breed Show that is usually confined to a single breed. The Kennel Club determines which breeds at which Championship Shows will have the opportunity to earn Challenge Certificates (or tickets). Serious exhibitors often will opt not to participate if the tickets are withheld at a particular show. This policy makes earning championships even more difficult to accomplish.

Open Shows are generally less competitive and are frequently used as 'practice shows' for young dogs. There are hundreds of Open Shows each year that can be delightful social events and are great first show experiences for the novice. Even if you're considering just watching a show to wet your paws, an Open Show is a great choice.

While Championship and Open Shows are most important for the beginner to understand, there are other types of shows in which the interested dog owner can participate. Training clubs sponsor Matches that can be entered on the day of the show for a nominal fee. In these introductory-level exhibitions, two dogs are pulled out of a hat and 'matched,' the winner of that match goes on to the next round, and eventually only one dog is left undefeated.

Exemption Shows are much more light-hearted affairs with

Champions compete with others for these coveted CCs. The number of Challenge Certificates awarded in any one year is based upon the total number of dogs in each breed entered for competition. There are three types of Championship Shows: an all-breed General Championship Show for all Kennel-Club-recognised breeds; a Group Championship Show that is limited to breeds within one of

usually only four pedigree classes and several 'fun' classes, all of which can be entered on the day. Exemption Shows are sometimes held in conjunction with small agricultural shows and the proceeds must be given to a charity. Limited Shows are also available in small number, but entry is restricted to members of the club which hosts the show, although one can usually join the club when making an entry.

Before you actually step into the ring, you would be well advised to sit back and observe the judge's ring procedure. If it is your first time in the ring, do not be over-anxious and run to the front of the line. It is much better to stand back and study how the exhibitor in front of you is performing. The judge asks each handler to 'stand' the dog, hopefully showing the dog off to his best advantage. The judge will observe the dog from a distance and from different angles, approach the dog, check his teeth, overall structure, alertness and muscle tone, as well as consider how well the dog 'conforms' to the standard. Most importantly, the judge will have the exhibitor move the dog around the ring in some pattern that he or she should specify (another advantage to not going first, but always listen since some judges change their directions, and the judge is always right!). Finally the judge

PRACTISE AT HOME

If you have decided to show your dog, you must train him to gait around the ring by your side at the correct pace and pattern, and to tolerate being handled and examined by the judge. Most breeds require complete dentition, all require a particular bite (scissor, level or undershot), and all males must have two apparently normal testicles fully descended into the scrotum. Enlist family and friends to hold mock trials in your garden to prepare your future champion!

will give the dog one last look before moving on to the next exhibitor.

If you are not in the top three

CLASSES AT DOG SHOWS

There can be as many as 18 classes per sex for your breed. Check the show schedule carefully to make sure that you have entered your dog in the appropriate class. Among the classes offered can be: Beginners; Minor Puppy (ages 6 to 9 months); Puppy (ages 6 to 12 months); Junior (ages 6 to 18 months); Beginners (handler or dog never won first place) as well as the following, each of which is defined in the schedule: Maiden; Novice; Tyro; Debutant; Undergraduate; Graduate; Postgraduate; Minor Limit; Mid Limit; Limit; Open; Veteran; Stud Dog; Brood Bitch; Progeny; Brace and Team.

at your first show, do not be discouraged. Be patient and consistent and you may eventually find yourself in the winning line-up. Remember that the winners were once in your shoes and have devoted many hours and

much money to earn the placement. If you find that your dog is losing every time and never getting a nod, it may be time to consider a different dog sport or just enjoy your Puli as a pet.

WORKING TRIALS

Working trials can be entered by any well-trained dog of any breed, not just Gundogs or Working dogs. Many dogs that earn the Kennel Club Good Citizen Dog award choose to participate in a working trial. There are five stakes at both open and championship levels: Companion Dog (CD), Utility Dog (UD), Working Dog (WD), Tracking Dog (TD) and Patrol Dog (PD). As in conformation shows, dogs compete against a standard and if the dog reaches the qualifying mark, it obtains a certificate. Divided into groups, each exercise must be achieved 70 percent in order for the dog to qualify. If the dog achieves 80 percent in the open level, it receives a Certificate

TEMPERAMENT PLUS

Although it seems that physical conformation is the only factor considered in the show ring, temperament is also of utmost importance. An aggressive or fearful dog should not be shown, as bad behaviour will not be tolerated and may pose a threat to the judge, other exhibitors, you and your dog.

SHOW RING ETIQUETTE

Just as with anything else, there is a certain etiquette to the show ring that can only be learned through experience. Showing your dog can be quite intimidating to you as a novice when it seems as if everyone else knows what they are doing. You can familiarise yourself with ring procedure beforehand by taking a class to prepare you and your dog for conformation showing or by talking with an experienced handler. When you are in the ring, listen and pay attention to the judge and follow his/her directions. Remember, even the most skilled handlers had to start somewhere. Keep it up and you too will become a proficient handler before too long!

of Merit (COM); in the championship level, it receives a Qualifying Certificate. At the CD stake, dogs must participate in four groups: Control, Stay, Agility and Search (Retrieve and Nosework). At the next three levels, UD, WD and TD, there are only three groups: Control, Agility and Nosework.

Agility consists of three jumps: a vertical scale up a six-foot wall of planks; a clear jump over a basic three-foot hurdle with a removable top bar; and a long jump across angled planks stretching nine feet.

To earn the UD, WD and TD, dogs must track approximately one-half mile for articles laid from one-half hour to three hours previously. Tracks consist of turns and legs, and fresh ground is used for each participant. The fifth stake, PD, involves teaching manwork, which is not recommended for every breed.

FIELD TRIALS AND WORKING TESTS

Working tests are frequently used to prepare dogs for field trials, the purpose of which is to heighten the instincts and natural abilities of Gundogs. Live game is not used in working tests. Unlike field trials, working tests do not count toward a dog's record at The Kennel Club, though the same judges often oversee working tests. Field trials began in England in 1947 and are only moderately

Ch Weetoneon the Equalizer, owned by Lacey Szyczewski, is a Working Group winner as well as a champion.

The world's oldest dog show is the Westminster Kennel Club Dog Show, which takes place annually in New York City. The group finals are completely televised on national broadcasts. About 50,000 people per day attend the show.

popular amongst dog folk. While breeders of Working and Gundog breeds concern themselves with the field abilities of their dogs, there is considerably less interest in field trials than in dog shows. In order for dogs to become full Champions, certain breeds must qualify in the field as well. Upon gaining three CCs in the show ring, the dog is designated a Show Champion (Sh Ch). The title Champion (Ch) requires that the dog gain an award at a field trial, be a 'special qualifier' at a field trial or pass a 'special show dog qualifier' judged by a field trial judge on a shooting day.

AGILITY TRIALS

Agility trials began in the United Kingdom in 1977 and have since spread around the world, especially to the United States, where they are very popular. The handler directs his dog over an obstacle course that includes jumps (such as those used in the working trials), as well as tyres, the dog walk, weave poles, pipe tunnels, collapsed tunnels, etc. The Kennel Club requires that dogs not be trained for agility until they are 12 months old. This dog sport is great fun for dog and owner and interested owners should join a training club that has obstacles and experienced agility handlers who can introduce you and your dog to the 'ropes' (and tyres, tunnels, etc.).

FÉDÉRATION CYNOLOGIQUE INTERNATIONALE

Established in 1911, the Fédération Cynologique Internationale (FCI) represents the 'world kennel club.' This international body brings uniformity to the breeding, judging and showing of purebred dogs. Although the FCI originally included only five European nations: France, Germany, Austria, the Netherlands and Belgium (which remains its headquarters), the organisation today embraces nations on six continents and recognises well over 300 breeds of purebred dog. There are three titles attainable through the FCI: the International Champion, which is the most prestigious; the International Beauty Champion, which is based on aptitude certificates in

FCI INFORMATION

There are 330 breeds recognised by the FCI, and each breed is considered to be 'owned' by a specific country. Each breed standard is a cooperative effort between the breed's country and the FCI's Standards and Scientific Commissions. Judges use these official breed standards at shows held in FCI member countries. One of the functions of the FCI is to update and translate the breed standards into French, English, Spanish and German.

different countries; and the International Trial Champion, which is based on achievement in obedience trials in different countries. Dogs from every country can participate in these impressive canine spectacles, the largest of which is the World Dog Show, hosted in a different country each year. FCI sponsors both national and international shows. The hosting country determines the judging system and breed standards are always based on the breed's country of origin.

The FCI is divided into ten 'Groups.' At the World Dog Show, the following 'Classes' are offered for each breed: Puppy Class (6–9 months), Youth Class (9–18 months), Open Class (15 months or older) and Champion Class. A dog can be awarded a classification of Excellent, Very Good, Good, Sufficient and Not Sufficient. Puppies can be awarded classifications of Very Promising, Promising or Not Promising. Four placements are made in each class. After all sexes and classes are judged, a Best of Breed is selected. Other special groups and classes may also be shown. Each exhibitor showing a dog receives a written evaluation from the judge.

Besides the World Dog Show, you can exhibit your dog at speciality shows held by different breed clubs. Speciality shows may have their own regulations.

TIDINESS COUNTS

Surely you've spent hours grooming your dog to perfection for the show ring, but don't forget about yourself! While the dog should be the centre of attention, it is important that you also appear clean and tidy. Wear smart, appropriate clothes and comfortable shoes in a colour that contrasts with your dog's coat. Look and act like a professional.

INDEX

*Page numbers in **boldface** indicate illustrations.*

My Hungarian Puli

PUT YOUR PUPPY'S FIRST PICTURE HERE

Dog's Name _____

Date _____ Photographer _____